# Cougars (

## *Keighley Cougars*
## *Year.*

# Edited by David Kirkley

## London League Publications Ltd

# Cougars Going Up!
## Keighley Cougars Rugby League 2003 Yearbook

© Copyright David Kirkley and contributors.
The moral right of David Kirkley and the contributors to be identified as the author has been asserted.

Cover design © Stephen McCarthy.

Photographs: Trevor Smith unless credited otherwise. © copyright to the photographer.

A CIP catalogue record for this book is available from the British Library.

First published in Great Britain in February 2004 by:
London League Publications Ltd, P.O. Box 10441, London E14 0SB

ISBN:                     1-903659-15-9

Cover design:             Stephen McCarthy Graphic Design
                          46, Clarence Road, London N15 5BB

Layout:                   Peter Lush

Printed and bound by:     Biddles Ltd, King's Lynn, Great Britain

**David Kirkley's share of the profits from this book will be used to support the development of the Keighley Cougars Academy.**

For more information about other books from London League Publications Ltd, visit our website: www.llpshop.co.uk
or write for a free catalogue to us at:
PO Box 10441, London E14 0SB

# Acknowledgements

Special thanks to John Pitchford for his encyclopaedic knowledge of the Keighley club, his immense contribution to this book and tremendous support. Thanks also to John Doveston for his guiding input into the project; also for help advice and encouragement to Rob Grillo and to John Huxley and the Rugby Football League for permission to use the tables and results which are copyright of the RFL; to Trevor Smith for kindly allowing use to use some of his always-excellent photographs; to *The Keighley News* for permission to reprint the 1903 match report; to Roger Pitchford and Clive Harrison for help with the league tables and results, to Eric Farr for information on the first season; to Trevor Delaney and Robert Gate for their help and to Ann Self for her help in compiling the diary.

And finally, thank you to Dave Farrar and Peter Lush from London League Publications Ltd for their work in publishing the book.

**David Kirkley**

## About the writers

**David Kirkley** has been a Cougars fan for many years and comes from a rugby family with his dad Allan and brother Don playing for the Keighley club. He has been involved with the Cougars Hall of Fame as well as being programme editor.

**John Pitchford** is a mine of information about rugby league especially Keighley. He has not missed a game home or away for over 25 years and was once in the running for rugby league fan of the year.

# Keighley Cougars club records

| | | | |
|---|---|---|---|
| Biggest Home Win | 86-0 | 1-11-1992 | -v- Nottingham City |
| Biggest Away Win | 104-4 | 23-04-1995 | -v- Highfield (at Rochdale) |
| Biggest Home Defeat | 0-76 | 15-02-1998 | -v- Wigan |
| Biggest Away Defeat | 2-92 | 03-04-1986 | -v- Leigh |
| Highest Attendance | 14,500 | 03-03-1951 | -v- Halifax |
| Lowest Attendance | 216 | 04-04-1987 | -v- Fulham |

## Players Match Records

| | | | |
|---|---|---|---|
| *Points in a match* | 36 | John Wasyliw –v- Nottingham City | 31-10-1993 |
| *Goals in a match* | 15 | John Wasyliw –v-Nottingham City | 01-11-1992 |
| | 15 | Martin Wood –v- Lancashire Lynx | 01-05-2000 |
| *Tries in a match* | 6 | Jason Critchley –v- Widnes | 18-08-1996 |
| *1 point drop-goals in a match* | 3 | Colin North –v- Whitehaven | 28-09-1980 |
| | 3 | Paul Moses –v- Huddersfield | 26-03-1986 |
| | 3 | Jason Ramshaw –v- Barrow | 30-01-1994 |

## Players' individual season records

| | | |
|---|---|---|
| *Points in a Season* | 490 John Wasyliw | 1992-93 season |
| *Goals in a Season* | 187 John Wasyliw | 1992-93 season |
| *Tries in a Season* | 45 Nick Pinkney | 1994-95 season |
| *One- point drop goals in a season* | 16 Colin North | 1980-81 season |

## Players' individual career records

| | | |
|---|---|---|
| Points: | 2,116 Brian Jefferson | 1965-77 |
| Goals: | 967 Brian Jefferson | 1965-77 |
| Tries: | 155 Sam Stacey | 1903-20 |
| One-point drop-goals: | 28 Colin North | 1980-84 |
| | 28 Paul Moses | 1984-94 |
| Appearances: | 372 Hartley Tempest | 1902-15 |
| | 372 Dave McGouan | 1925-38 |
| Consecutive appearances: | 154 Cyril Halliday (Aug 1935 - Feb 1939) | |
| Consecutive scoring appearances: | 46 John Wasyliw (Feb 1992 – Sept 1993) | |
| | (238 goals, 37 tries) | |
| Consecutive try scoring appearances: | 8 Nick Pinkney (19 tries) (Oct - Dec 1994) | |

# Contents

Cougars' head coach Gary Moorby

# 1. 2003 Season Review

It was a season of tremendous progress for Keighley Cougars who failed the previous season to make the cut in a one division Northern Ford Premiership and consequently found themselves in the lower professional division of the new National League Two. Conversely this turned out to be positive, as it gave Cougars time to carry on the rebuilding they had started the previous season.

Coaches Gary Moorby and Paul Moses assembled a good squad, which was kept at an excellent level of fitness by Paul Royston. Key established players such as Jason Ramshaw, Phil Stephenson, Matt Firth and James Rushforth had good seasons. On top of this a wealth of young squad members integrated well into team. In particular the return of Matt Foster in March had a big impact.

The season started extremely well with a good win over National League One side Doncaster in the Arriva Trains Cup. After this a run of three losses in the competition suggested that Cougars would not progress into the play-offs. Then four wins out of the next five games propelled the club into a position where a win at Batley was needed to progress. This did not happen but then it was down to National League Two matters.

A run of seven straight victories saw Cougars topping the table and it was not until June when they came up against what was to prove their 'bogey team' Sheffield Eagles that the first league points were dropped. Cougars hit a bad spell in July with just two wins out of the next five games and they dropped to fourth position in the league. Showing the mettle of the squad they then picked themselves up and won four of their next five games in the season's run-in to finish third, on equal points with Sheffield and Chorley above them.

When the team romped home against Hunslet and Barrow at Cougar Park in the elimination play-offs, something special was in the air and an astonishing 45-12 win at Chorley underlined this. Then followed a mouth-watering Grand Final against Sheffield. The rest is history with Cougars winning the first half of the game and Sheffield storming out in the second but Cougars going in for the winning try late in the half. For those who picked up the pieces of the club from the ashes it was sweet indeed and just reward.

1

Back row (left to right) Chris Hannah, Karl Smith, Phil Stephenson, Oliver Wilkes, Phil Guck, Michael Durham. Middle Row (left to right) David Marshall (kit man), Colin Farrar (Director), Lee Patterson, Chris Wainwright, Richard Merville, Ian Sinfield, Max Tomlinson, Andy Robinson, Ricky Helliwell, Gary Moorby (Coach), Paul Royston (conditioner), Neil Spencer (Director). Front Row (left to right) Danny Ekis, Paul Ashton, James Rushforth, Adam Mitchell, Matt Firth.
(Insets) Matt Foster, Jason Ramshaw.

Cougars' assistant coach Paul Moses

2

***Date:*** **Sunday 19 January**                    ***At:*** **Cougar Park**
*Competition:* Arriva Trains Cup
*Opponents:* Doncaster Dragons          *Result* Won 21-14 (ht 12-10)
Cougars, superbly led by Jason Ramshaw, completely outplayed and out-fought the Dragons for a shock win which started with a mass brawl in the second minute.
*Team:* 1. James Rushforth, 2. Karl Smith, 3. David Foster, 4. Gareth Hewitt,
5. Andy Robinson, 6. Paul Ashton, 7. Matt Firth, 8. Phil Stephenson, 9. Simeon Hoyle,
10. Danny Ekis, 11. Ian Sinfield, 12. Ricky Helliwell, 13. Jason Ramshaw.
*Subs:* 14. Chris Wainwright, 15. Lee Patterson (dnp), 16. Oliver Wilkes, 17. Chris Hannah.
*Tries:* Robinson, Ashton, Helliwell.
*Goals:* Ashton (4). *Drop Goals:* Ashton
*Referee:* Steve Ganson                    *Attendance:* 1,337

***Date:***                              **Sunday 26 January       At:**
**Cougar Park**
*Competition:* TXU Energi Challenge Cup
*Opponents:* Thornhill Trojans           *Result:* Won 33-10 (ht 20-0)
Held by their lowly amateur opponents for spells Cougars score tries at key points in the game to take them into the next round of the cup.
*Team:* 1. James Rushforth, 2. Karl Smith, 3. David Foster, 4. Gareth Hewitt,
5. Andy Robinson, 6. Paul Ashton, 7. Matt Firth, 8. Phil Stephenson, 9. Simeon Hoyle,
10. Danny Ekis, 11. Ian Sinfield, 12. Ricky Helliwell, 13. Jason Ramshaw.
*Subs:* 14. Chris Wainwright, 15. Lee Patterson, 16. Oliver Wilkes, 17. Chris Hannah.
*Tries:* Ashton (2) Hoyle, Firth, Smith
*Goals:* Ashton (6). *Drop Goals:* Ashton
*Referee:* Ashley Klein                    *Attendance:* 1,135

***Date:***                              **Sunday 2 February       At:**
**Ram Stadium, Dewsbury** *Competition* Arriva Trains Cup
*Opponents* Dewsbury Rams                *Result* Lost 6-12 (ht 0-12)
In appalling conditions Cougars just fail to edge this hard fought game despite pressuring the Rams defence well in the second period.
*Team:* 1. James Rushforth, 2. Phil Guck, 3. Gareth Hewitt, 4. Chris Wainwright,
5. Andy Robinson, 6. Paul Ashton, 7. Matt Firth, 8. Phil Stephenson, 9. Simeon Hoyle,
10. Chris Hannah, 11. Dave Foster, 12. Ricky Helliwell, 13. Jason Ramshaw.
*Subs:* 14. Matthew Steel, 15. Oliver Wilkes, 16. Lee Kelly, 17. Danny Ekis.
*Try:* Rushforth.
*Goal:* Ashton.
*Referee:* Peter Taberner                    *Attendance:* 954

3

**Date:** Sunday 9 February                    **At:** Don Valley, Sheffield
*Competition:* TXU Energi Challenge Cup
*Opponents:* Sheffield Eagles              *Result:* Lost 24-25 (ht 8-12)
A desperately close match won in the last minute by a Richard Goddard drop-goal breaks Cougars hearts after they had fought back so well to get on equal terms.
*Team:* 1. James Rushforth, 2. Karl Smith, 3. David Foster, 4. Gareth Hewitt,
5. Andy Robinson, 6. Paul Ashton, 7. Matt Firth, 8. Phil Stephenson, 9. Simeon Hoyle,
10. Oliver Wilkes, 11. Ian Sinfield, 12. Ricky Helliwell, 13. Jason Ramshaw.
Subs: 14. Chris Wainwright, 15. Danny Ekis, 16. Matthew Steel (dnp), 17. Chris Hannah.
*Tries:* Hoyle, Smith, Sinfield, Wainwright, Rushforth
*Goals:* Ashton (2).
*Referee:* Steve Addy                      *Attendance:* 1,235

**Date:** Sunday 16 February                  **At:** Cougar Park
*Competition:* Arriva Trains Cup
*Opponents:* Batley Bulldogs               *Result:* Lost 12-30 (ht4-14)
A poor performance by Keighley sees Bulldogs take the points controlling the play for much of the match and playing for a good spell with 12 men.
*Team:* 1. James Rushforth, 2. Karl Smith, 3. Dave Foster, 4. Matthew Steel, 5. Phil Guck, 6. Adam Mitchell, 7. Matt Firth, 8. Phil Stephenson, 9. Simeon Hoyle, 10. Lee Kelly,
11. Oliver Wilkes, 12. Ian Sinfield, 13 Lee Patterson.
Subs: 14. Paul Ashton, 15. Danny Ekis, 16. Chris Wainwright, 17. Chris Hannah.
*Tries:* Smith, Rushforth.
*Goals:* Mitchell (2).
*Referee:* Steve Presley                    *Attendance:* 1,209

**Date:** Sunday 23 February                  **At:** South Leeds Stadium
*Competition:* Arriva Trains Cup
*Opponents:* Hunslet Hawks                *Result:* Lost 4-16 (ht4-10)
A frustrating game with both teams fairly clueless and Cougars failing to capitalise on Jason Ramshaw's kicking game.
*Team:* 1. James Rushforth, 2. Karl Smith, 3. Dave Foster, 4. Chris Wainwright,
5. Andy Robinson, 6. Paul Ashton, 7. Matt Firth, 8. Phil Stephenson, 9. Simeon Hoyle,
10. Danny Ekis, 11. Oliver Wilkes, 12. Ian Sinfield, 13 Jason Ramshaw.
Subs: 14 Lee Patterson, 15. Richard Merville, 16. Lee Kelly, 17. Chris Hannah.
*Goals:* Ashton (2).
*Referee:* Julian King                      *Attendance:* 610

4

**Date:** Sunday 9 March　　　　　　**At:** Cougar Park
*Competition:* Arriva Trains Cup
*Opponents:* London Skolars　　　　　*Result:* Won 78-18 (ht 38-0)
A 14-try demolition of Skolars gave Cougars a boost in a workmanlike performance and return to form. Matt Foster returned to the side.
*Team:* 1. James Rushforth, 2. Karl Smith, 3. Dave Foster, 4. Matt Foster,
5. Andy Robinson, 6. Paul Ashton, 7. Matt Firth, 8. Phil Stephenson, 9. Simeon Hoyle,
10. Danny Ekis, 11. Oliver Wilkes, 12. Ian Sinfield, 13 Jason Ramshaw.
Subs: 14 Chris Wainwright, 15. Gareth Hewitt, 16. Richard Merville,
17. Ricky Helliwell.
*Tries:* Firth (4), Ramshaw (2), Matt Foster (2), Smith (2), Merville, Hoyle, Wilkes, Robinson.
*Goals:* Ashton (8), Wilkes (3).
*Referee:* Steve Addy　　　　　　　*Attendance:* 732

**Date:** Sunday 16 March　　　　　　**At:** Cougar Park
*Competition:* Arriva Trains Cup
*Opponents:* Dewsbury Rams　　　　　*Result:* Won 22-2 (ht8-0)
Cougars built on the previous week's performance, being strong in defence and clever in attack to overwhelm Rams. Matt Firth was outstanding.
*Team:* 1. James Rushforth, 2. Karl Smith, 3. Dave Foster, 4. Matt Foster,
5. Andy Robinson, 6. Adam Mitchell, 7. Matt Firth, 8. Phil Stephenson,
9. Simeon Hoyle, 10. Danny Ekis, 11. Oliver Wilkes, 12. Ian Sinfield,
13. Jason Ramshaw.
Subs: 14 Chris Wainwright, 15. Gareth Hewitt, 16. Ricky Helliwell,
17. Richard Merville.
*Tries:* Firth, Robinson, Mitchell, Wainwright.
*Goals:* Mitchell (3).
*Referee:* Peter Taberner　　　　　　*Attendance:* 1,111

**Date:** Sunday 23 March　　　　　　**At:** Belle Vue, Doncaster
*Competition:* Arriva Trains Cup
*Opponents:* Doncaster Dragons　　　*Result:* Lost 12-42 (ht 12-10)
After leading at half-time Cougars are outplayed in the second period with a six try blitz by Dragons.
*Team:* 1. James Rushforth, 2. Karl Smith, 3. Dave Foster, 4. Gareth Hewitt,
5. Andy Robinson, 6. Adam Mitchell, 7. Matt Firth, 8. Phil Stephenson,
9. Simeon Hoyle, 10. Danny Ekis, 11. Oliver Wilkes, 12. Ian Sinfield,
13. Jason Ramshaw.
Subs: 14 Chris Wainwright, 15. Ricky Helliwell, 16. Richard Merville,
17. Chris Hannah.
*Tries:* Firth (2)
*Goals:* Mitchell (2)
*Referee:* Colin Morris　　　　　　　*Attendance:* 985

Matt Firth had another great season at
half-back and never missed a game.

**Date:** Sunday 30 March          **At:** New River Stadium

*Competition:* Arriva Trains Cup

*Opponents:* London Skolars        *Result:* Won 48-18 (ht 20-10)

Keighley started well, but survived a scare by Skolars who scored three tries around the break and came within two points. Cougars finished well with four tries to take the game.

*Team:* 1. James Rushforth, 2. Karl Smith, 3. Dave Foster, 4. Gareth Hewitt,
5. Andy Robinson, 6. Adam Mitchell, 7. Matt Firth, 8. Phil Stephenson,
9. Simeon Hoyle, 10. Danny Ekis, 11. Oliver Wilkes, 12. Ricky Helliwell,
13 Lee Patterson.

Subs: 14 Chris Wainwright, 15. Ian Sinfield, 16. Mick Durham, 17. Chris Hannah.

*Tries:* Patterson, Hewitt (2), Stephenson, Helliwell, Wilkes, Robinson, Durham.

*Goals:* Mitchell (8).

*Referee:* Julian King          *Attendance:* 310

**Date:** Sunday 6 April          **At:** Cougar Park

*Competition:* Arriva Trains Cup

*Opponents:* Hunslet Hawks        *Result:* Won 21-8 (ht 16-2)

A hard-fought win set up a fascinating final game in the group. Cougars were big in defence and clinical in attack. Matt Firth was superb.

*Team:* 1. James Rushforth, 2. Karl Smith, 3. Dave Foster, 4. Gareth Hewitt,
5. Andy Robinson, 6. Adam Mitchell, 7. Matt Firth, 8. Phil Stephenson,
9. Simeon Hoyle, 10. Danny Ekis, 11. Oliver Wilkes, 12. Ricky Helliwell,
13. Jason Ramshaw.

Subs: 14. Chris Wainwright, 15. Matt Foster, 16. Ian Sinfield, 17. Chris Hannah.

*Tries:* Dave Foster, Hoyle, Robinson.

*Goals:* Mitchell (4)

*Drop Goal:* Firth

*Referee:* Ben Thaler          *Attendance:* 1,170

**Date:** Sunday 13 April          **At:** Mount Pleasant, Batley

*Competition:* Arriva Trains Cup

*Opponents:* Batley Bulldogs        *Result:* Lost 16-40 (ht 10-16)

Cougars' cup hopes were crushed by Bulldogs though the score flatters Bulldogs in a game closer than the result suggests.

*Team:* 1. James Rushforth, 2. Karl Smith, 3. Dave Foster, 4. Matt Foster,
5. Andy Robinson, 6. Adam Mitchell, 7. Matt Firth, 8. Phil Stephenson,
9. Simeon Hoyle, 10. Chris Hannah, 11. Oliver Wilkes, 12. Ricky Helliwell,
13. Jason Ramshaw.

Subs: 15. Richard Merville, 16. Gareth Hewitt, 17. Danny Ekis.

*Tries:* Matt Foster, Rushforth, Wilkes

*Goals:* Mitchell (2)

*Referee:* Ashley Klein          *Attendance:* 737

7

**Date:** Friday 18 April                    **At:** South Leeds Stadium
*Competition:* National League Division Two
*Opponents:* Hunslet Hawks                    *Result:* Won 20-12 (ht 8-0)
A fine away win signals Keighley's credentials for the coming season in the first league game. Simeon Hoyle and Ricky Helliwell put in fine performances.
*Team:* 1. James Rushforth, 2. Karl Smith, 3. Dave Foster, 4. Gareth Hewitt,
5. Andy Robinson, 6. Adam Mitchell, 7. Matt Firth, 8. Chris Hannah, 9. Simeon Hoyle,
10. Danny Ekis, 11. Oliver Wilkes, 12. Ricky Helliwell, 13 Jason Ramshaw.
Subs: 14. Chris Wainwright, 16. Richard Merville, 17. Ian Sinfield.
*Tries:* Hewitt, Dave Foster, Wainwright
*Goals:* Mitchell (4)
*Referee:* Ashley Klein          *Attendance:* 607          *League Position:* 1

**Date:** Sunday 21 April                    **At:** Cougar Park
*Competition:* National League Division Two
*Opponents:* London Skolars                    *Result:* Won 68-6 (ht 46-0)
A 13-try romp sees Cougars do a thoroughly professional job over division strugglers London. Jason Ramshaw was central in most of Keighley's moves.
*Team:* 1. James Rushforth, 2. Karl Smith, 3. Dave Foster, 4. Chris Wainwright,
5. Max Tomlinson, 6. Paul Ashton, 7. Matt Firth, 8. Chris Hannah, 9. Simeon Hoyle,
10. Lee Kelly, 11. Oliver Wilkes, 12. Lee Patterson, 13 Jason Ramshaw.
Subs: 14. Gareth Hewitt, 15. Ian Sinfield, 16. Danny Ekis, 17. Richard Merville.
*Tries:* Rushforth (4), Patterson (2), Smith, Wilkes (2), Ekis (2), Tomlinson, Firth.
*Goals:* Ashton (7), Wilkes
*Referee:* Steve Addy          *Attendance:* 963          *League Position:* 1

**Date:** Sunday 4 May                    **At:** Victory Park, Chorley
*Competition:* National League Division Two
*Opponents:* Chorley Lynx                    *Result:* Won 23-22 (ht 6-16)
Chorley let skip a ten-point half time lead when Cougars' character sees them through with a top second half performance to take the points.
*Team:* 1. James Rushforth, 2. Karl Smith, 3. Dave Foster, 4. Matt Foster,
5. Gareth Hewitt, 6. Adam Mitchell, 7. Matt Firth, 8. Phil Stephenson, 9. Simeon Hoyle,
10. Danny Ekis, 11. Oliver Wilkes, 12. Ricky Helliwell, 13 Jason Ramshaw.
Subs: 14. Ashton (dnp), 15. Lee Patterson, 16. Ian Sinfield, 17. Richard Merville.
*Tries:* Hewitt (2), Matt Foster (2)
*Goals:* Mitchell (3) *Drop Goal:* Firth
*Referee:* Mike Dawber          *Attendance:* 501          *League Position:* 1

8

**Date:** Sunday 11 May        **At:** Cougar Park
*Competition:* National League Division Two
*Opponents:* York City Knights      *Result:* Won 38-26 (ht 26-0)
A big half time lead gave Cougars a platform for the win, but the team disappointed in the second half. Once again Ramshaw ran the game.
*Team:* 1. James Rushforth, 2. Gareth Hewitt, 3. Dave Foster, 4. Matt Foster,
5. Andy Robinson, 6. Adam Mitchell, 7. Matt Firth, 8. Phil Stephenson,
9. Simeon Hoyle, 10. Danny Ekis, 11. Oliver Wilkes, 12. Ian Sinfield,
13. Jason Ramshaw.
Subs: 14. Chris Wainwright, 15. Ricky Helliwell, 16.Richard Merville,
17. Chris Hannah.
*Tries:* Dave Foster, Matt Foster (2), Rushforth, Hoyle, Hewitt
*Goals:* Mitchell (7)
*Referee:* Steve Nicholson     *Attendance:* 1,077     *League Position:* 1

**Date:** Sunday 25 May        **At:** Derwent Park
*Competition:* National League Division Two
*Opponents:* Workington Town      *Result:* Won 44-8 (ht 10-4)
A big second half performance saw Cougars score 34 points after the break. Adam Mitchell headed a superb half-back partnership.
*Team:* 1. James Rushforth, 2. Gareth Hewitt, 3. Dave Foster, 4. Matt Foster,
5. Andy Robinson, 6. Adam Mitchell, 7. Matt Firth, 8. Phil Stephenson
9. Simeon Hoyle, 10. Danny Ekis, 11. Oliver Wilkes, 12. Ian Sinfield,
13. Jason Ramshaw.
Subs: 14. Chris Wainwright, 15. Lee Patterson, 16.Richard Merville, 17 Mick Durham.
*Tries:* Robinson (2), Ramshaw, Matt Foster (2), Dave Foster, Hoyle
*Goals:* Mitchell (8)
*Referee:* Julian King     *Attendance:* 610     *League Position:* 1

**Date:** Sunday 1 June        **At:** Cougar Park
*Competition:* National League Division Two
*Opponents:* Barrow Raiders      *Result:* Won 28-15 (ht 22-3)
Cougars made it six wins out of six with a fine performance headed by game star Ollie Wilkes. Cougars did enough in the first half to take the points.
*Team:* 1. James Rushforth, 2. Karl Smith, 3. Dave Foster, 4. Matt Foster,
5. Andy Robinson, 6. Adam Mitchell, 7. Matt Firth, 8. Phil Stephenson,
9. Simeon Hoyle, 10. Danny Ekis, 11. Oliver Wilkes, 12. Ian Sinfield,
13. Jason Ramshaw.
Subs: 14. Chris Wainwright. 15. Lee Patterson, 16.Richard Merville, 17, Mick Durham.

*Tries:* Wilkes, Dave Foster, Robinson, Firth, Wainwright
*Goals:* Mitchell (4)
*Referee:* Steve Presley     *Attendance:* 1,106     *League Position:* 1

*Date:* **Sunday 15 June**  *At:* **Cougar Park**
*Competition:* National League Division Two
*Opponents:* Gateshead Thunder  *Result:* Won 52-6 (ht 22-6)
An eager, but outclassed Thunder side were comfortably beaten by Cougars now on a roll. Matt Firth bagged a hat-trick and Simeon Hoyle two tries.
*Team:* 1. James Rushforth, 2. Karl Smith, 3. Dave Foster, 4. Matt Foster,
5. Andy Robinson, 6. Adam Mitchell, 7. Matt Firth, 8. Phil Stephenson,
9. Simeon Hoyle, 10. Danny Ekis, 11. Oliver Wilkes, 12. Ian Sinfield,
13. Jason Ramshaw.
Subs: 14. Paul Ashton, 15. Lee Patterson, 16.Mick Durham, 17. Chris Hannah.
*Tries:* Mitchell, Matt Foster (2), Hoyle (2), Firth (3), Ramshaw (2)
*Goals:* Mitchell (4), Ashton (2)
*Referee:* Ben Thaler  *Attendance:* 992  *League Position:* 1

*Date:* **Sunday 22 June**  *At:* **Don Valley Stadium**
*Competition:* National League Division Two
*Opponents:* Sheffield Eagles  *Result:* Lost 6-33 (ht 0-24)
Another rough tough game saw Cougars suffer their first defeat of the League season against the side that were to trouble them all year.
*Team:* 1. James Rushforth, 2. Gareth Hewitt, 3. Dave Foster, 4. Andy Robinson,
5. Matt Foster, 6. Adam Mitchell, 7. Matt Firth, 8. Phil Stephenson, 9. Simeon Hoyle,
10. Danny Ekis, 11. Oliver Wilkes, 12. Ian Sinfield, 13 Jason Ramshaw.
Subs: 14. Chris Wainwright, 15. Lee Patterson, 16.Ricky Helliwell,
17. Richard Merville.
*Try:* Ramshaw
*Goal:* Wilkes
*Referee:* Julian King  *Attendance:* 1,126  *League Position:* 1

*Date:* **Sunday 29 June**  *At:* **Cougar Park**
*Competition:* National League Division Two
*Opponents:* Swinton Lions  *Result:* Won 18-15 (ht 12-10)
Cougars were back to winning ways with a late try by Matt Foster to take the points after trailing for most of the second half to a spirited Swinton side.
*Team:* 1. James Rushforth, 2. Max Tomlinson, 3. Dave Foster, 4. Matt Foster,
5. Andy Robinson, 6. Adam Mitchell, 7. Matt Firth, 8. Phil Stephenson,
9. Simeon Hoyle, 10. Ian Sinfield, 11. Oliver Wilkes, 12. Ricky Helliwell, 13. Jason Ramshaw.
Subs: 14. Paul Ashton, 15. Mick Durham, 16.Danny Ekis, 17. Chris Hannah.
*Tries:* Wilkes, Tomlinson, Matt Foster
*Goals:* Mitchell (2), Ashton
*Referee:* Clive Walker  *Attendance:* 1,129  *League Position:* 1

**Date:** Sunday 13 July          **At: Huntington Stadium**
*Competition:* National League Division Two
*Opponents:* York City Knights        *Result:* Lost 28-48 (ht 10-14)
A patchy performance by Cougars saw them lose ground to divisional chasers with a superb performance by the home side.
*Team:* 1. James Rushforth, 2. Gareth Hewitt, 3. Chris Wainwright, 4. Matt Foster
5. Andy Robinson, 6. Adam Mitchell, 7. Matt Firth, 8. Chris Hannah, 9. Simeon Hoyle,
10. Ian Sinfield, 11. Oliver Wilkes, 12. David Foster, 13 Jason Ramshaw.
Subs: 14. Paul Ashton, 15. Lee Patterson, 16.Richard Merville, 17. Danny Ekis.
*Tries:* Rushforth, Mitchell, Robinson, Matt Foster, Dave Foster
*Goals:* Mitchell, Ashton (3)
*Referee:* Steve Presley      *Attendance:* 1,835      *League Position:* 1

**Date:** Sunday 20 July          **At: Cougar Park**
*Competition:* National League Division Two
*Opponents:* Chorley Lynx        *Result:* Lost 20-23 (ht 13-8)
A close game, but Cougars' below par performance saw them lose ground again in the division as the race for the top three heated up.
*Team:* 1. James Rushforth, 2. Karl Smith, 3. Dave Foster, 4. Matt Foster,
5. Andy Robinson, 6. Adam Mitchell, 7. Matt Firth, 8. Chris Hannah, 9. Simeon Hoyle,
10. Ian Sinfield, 11. Oliver Wilkes, 12. Lee Patterson, 13. Jason Ramshaw.
Subs: 14. Chris Wainwright, 15. Mick Durham, 16.Ricky Helliwell,
17. Richard Merville.
*Tries:* Matt Foster, Mitchell, Firth.
*Goals:* Mitchell (3).
*Drop Goals:* Firth (2).
*Referee:* Julian King      *Attendance:* 1,028      *League Position:* 1

**Date:** Sunday 27 July          **At: New River Stadium**
*Competition:* National League Division Two
*Opponents:* London Skolars        *Result:* Won 22-14 (ht 10-8)
A last minute try by Matt Foster saved Cougars' blushes when an excellent performance by the division's bottom club almost gave them their first win.
*Team:* 1. James Rushforth, 2. Karl Smith, 3. Dave Foster, 4. Matt Foster,
5. Andy Robinson, 6. Paul Ashton, 7. Matt Firth, 8. Chris Hannah, 9. Simeon Hoyle,
10. Danny Ekis, 11. Oliver Wilkes, 12. Ian Sinfield, 13 Jason Ramshaw.
Subs: 14. Chris Wainwright, 15. Lee Patterson, 16.Ricky Helliwell, 17. Richard Merville.
*Tries:* Wilkes, Matt Foster, Helliwell, Wainwright.
*Goals:* Ashton (3).
*Referee:* Ben Thaler      *Attendance:* 304      *League Position:* 1

Voted Supporters' Player-of-the-Year, Oliver Wilkes had an outstanding season for Cougars and here powers his way through the Hunslet Hawks' defence.

*Date:* **Sunday 3 August**                    *At:* **Cougar Park**
*Competition:* National League Division Two
*Opponents:* Hunslet Hawks          *Result:* Lost 18-35 (ht 14-16)
The mid-season slump continued for Keighley with a bad home defeat that saw them off the top of the table for the first time this season.
*Team:* 1. James Rushforth, 2. Karl Smith, 3. Dave Foster, 4. Matt Foster,
5. Andy Robinson, 6. Paul Ashton, 7. Matt Firth, 8. Phil Stephenson, 9. Simeon Hoyle,
10. Scott Parkin, 11. Oliver Wilkes, 12. Ian Sinfield, 13. Jason Ramshaw.
*Subs:* 14. Chris Wainwright, 15. Ricky Helliwell, 16. Danny Ekis, 17 Chris Hannah.
*Tries:* Hoyle, Firth, Robinson.
*Goals:* Ashton (3).
*Referee:* Andy Leonard        *Attendance:* 1,035      *League Position:* 4

*Date:* **Sunday 10 August**                    *At:* **Cougar Park**
*Competition:* National League Division Two
*Opponents:* Workington Town          *Result:* Won 35-6 (ht 19-0)
Cougars bounced back with a much-improved performance in a seven-try romp at home. Richard Merville had an outstanding performance as substitute.
*Team:* 1. Matt Foster, 2. Karl Smith, 3. Dave Foster, 4. Chris Wainwright,
5. Andy Robinson, 6. Paul Ashton, 7. Matt Firth, 8. Phil Stephenson, 9. Simeon Hoyle,
10. Scott Parkin, 11. Oliver Wilkes, 12. Ian Sinfield, 13 Jason Ramshaw.
*Subs:* 14. Adam Mitchell, 15. Ricky Helliwell, 16.Mick Durham, 17. Richard Merville.
*Tries:* Dave Foster, Wilkes, Wainwright, Helliwell, Mitchell, Sinfield, Matt Foster.
*Goals:* Ashton, Mitchell (3). *Drop Goal:* Ashton.
*Referee:* Ben Thaler        *Attendance:* 844      *League Position:* 3

*Date:* **Sunday 17 August**                    *At:* **Craven Park, Barrow**
*Competition:* National League Division Two
*Opponents:* Barrow Raiders          *Result:* Won 18-16 (ht 10-6)
A hard-worked win at Barrow kept Cougars in the title chase with a last-minute try by Andy Robinson.
*Team:* 1. Matt Foster, 2. Max Tomlinson, 3. Dave Foster, 4. Chris Wainwright,
5. Andy Robinson, 6. Adam Mitchell, 7. Matt Firth, 8. Phil Stephenson,
9. Ricky Helliwell, 10. Richard Merville, 11. Oliver Wilkes, 12. Ian Sinfield,
13. Jason Ramshaw.
*Subs:* 14. James Rushforth, 15. Lee Patterson, 16.Mick Durham, 17 Danny Ekis.
*Tries:* Robinson (2), Ramshaw, Dave Foster.
*Goals:* Mitchell.
*Referee:* Clive Walker        *Attendance:* 826      *League Position:* 2

13

**Date:** Sunday 24 August                **At:** Cougar Park
*Competition:* National League Division Two
*Opponents:* Sheffield Eagles         *Result:* Lost 10-22 (ht 10-2)
Eagles again blighted Cougars' title hopes with a strong second half performance, running in three tries.
*Team:* 1. Matt Foster, 2. Max Tomlinson, 3. Dave Foster, 4. Chris Wainwright, 5. Andy Robinson, 6. Adam Mitchell, 7. Matt Firth, 8. Phil Stephenson, 9. Mick Durham, 10. Richard Merville, 11. Oliver Wilkes, 12. Ian Sinfield, 13. Jason Ramshaw.
Subs: 14. James Rushforth, 15. Lee Patterson, 16.Ricky Helliwell, 17. Danny Ekis.
*Try:* Matt Foster.
*Goals:* Mitchell (3).
*Referee:* Steve Addy      *Attendance:* 1,468      *League Position:* 3

**Date:** Sunday 31 August           **At:** Moor Lane, Swinton
*Competition:* National League Division Two
*Opponents:* Swinton Lions           *Result:* Won 19-17 (ht 18-3)
Cougars ensured a play-off place with another gritty performance at Swinton. A strong first half ensured they had enough to take both points.
*Team:* 1. Matt Foster, 2. Max Tomlinson, 3. Dave Foster, 4. James Rushforth, 5. Andy Robinson, 6. Paul Ashton, 7. Matt Firth, 8. Phil Stephenson, 9. Simeon Hoyle, 10. Richard Merville, 11. Oliver Wilkes, 12. Ian Sinfield, 13 Jason Ramshaw.
Subs: 14. Lee Patterson, 15. Mick Durham, 16.Ricky Helliwell, 17. Scott Parkin.
*Tries:* Sinfield (2), Robinson.
*Goals:* Ashton (3), *Drop Goal:* Ashton.
*Referee:* Mick Dawber      *Attendance:* 507      *League Position:* 3

**Date:** Sunday 7 September         **At:** The Thunderdome
*Competition:* National League Division Two
*Opponents:* Gateshead Thunder     *Result:* Won 21-16 (ht 6-16)
Gateshead nearly spoiled Cougars' season end going in leading in the first half, but three second half tries gave Keighley a deserved win.
*Team:* 1. Matt Foster, 2. Max Tomlinson, 3. Dave Foster, 4. James Rushforth, 5. Andy Robinson, 6. Paul Ashton, 7. Matt Firth, 8. Phil Stephenson, 9. Simeon Hoyle, 10. Mick Durham, 11. Oliver Wilkes, 12. Ian Sinfield, 13. Jason Ramshaw.
Subs: 14. Karl Smith, 15. Lee Patterson, 16. Danny Ekis.
*Tries:* Dave Foster, Wilkes, Smith (2).
*Goals:* Ashton (2), *Drop Goal:* Ashton.
*Referee:* Steve Addy      *Attendance:* 349      *League Position:* 3

**Date:** Sunday 14 September          **At:** **Cougar Park**
*Competition:* National League Division Two (Elimination play-off)
*Opponents:* Hunslet Hawks          *Result:* Won 25-12 (ht 12-4)
Eight goal Paul Ashton, who hit a purple patch, is the difference in this game where both sides scored two tries. Cougars now on a hard worked run of five wins out of six.
*Team:* 1. Matt Foster, 2. Max Tomlinson, 3. Dave Foster, 4. James Rushforth,
5. Andy Robinson, 6. Paul Ashton, 7. Matt Firth, 8. Phil Stephenson, 9. Simeon Hoyle,
10. Danny Ekis, 11. Oliver Wilkes, 12. Ian Sinfield, 13 Lee Patterson.
Subs: 14. Chris Wainwright, 15. Jason Ramshaw, 16. Mick Durham,
17. Richard Merville.
*Tries:* Merville, Sinfield.
*Goals:*  Ashton (8), *Drop Goal:* Ashton.
*Referee:* Ronnie Laughton          *Attendance:* 1,150

**Date:** Sunday 21 September          **At:** **Cougar Park**
*Competition:* National League Division Two (Elimination semi-final)
*Opponents:* Barrow Raiders          *Result:* Won 35-26 (ht 13-0)
Ashton again was the inspiration with two tries and nine goals as Cougars easily outplayed the Raiders whose four late tries give the score an unrealistic look. Jason Ramshaw's last home game was rewarded with a touchdown near the posts.
*Team:* 1. Matt Foster, 2. Max Tomlinson, 3. Dave Foster, 4. James Rushforth,
5. Andy Robinson, 6. Paul Ashton, 7. Matt Firth, 8. Phil Stephenson, 9. Simeon Hoyle,
10. Danny Ekis, 11. Oliver Wilkes, 12. Ian Sinfield, 13 Lee Patterson.
Subs: 14. Chris Wainwright, 15.Richard Merville, 16. Mick Durham,
17. Jason Ramshaw.
*Tries:* Ashton (2), Ramshaw, Rushforth.
*Goals:*  Ashton (9), *Drop Goal:* Ashton.
*Referee:* Ronnie Laughton          *Attendance:* 1,332

**Date:** Sunday 28 September          **At:** **Victory Park, Chorley**
*Competition:* National League Division Two (Final Eliminator)
*Opponents:* Chorley Lynx          *Result:* Won 45-12 (ht 19-6)
The expected close encounter never materialised and again Ashton was the inspiration with 25 points taking Cougars to a deserved Grand Final.
*Team:* 1. Matt Foster, 2. Max Tomlinson, 3. Dave Foster, 4. James Rushforth,
5. Andy Robinson, 6. Paul Ashton, 7. Matt Firth, 8. Phil Stephenson, 9. Simeon Hoyle,
10. Danny Ekis, 11. Oliver Wilkes, 12. Ian Sinfield, 13 Lee Patterson.
Subs: 14. Chris Wainwright, 15.Richard Merville, 16. Mick Durham,
17. Jason Ramshaw.
*Tries:* Tomlinson, Stephenson, Ekis, Robinson, Merville, Ashton (2).
*Goals:*  Ashton (8), *Drop Goal:* Ashton.
*Referee:* Richard Silverwood          *Attendance:* 1,085

***Date:* Saturday 5 October**     ***At:* Halton Stadium, Widnes**
*Competition:* National League Division Two (Grand Final)
*Opponents:* Sheffield Eagles     *Result:* Won 13-11 (ht 9-4)
So the 'crunch' match against the Eagles who Cougars had not beaten all season. The first half was dominated by Cougars who went in 9-4 in the lead from a Matt Foster try converted by Paul Ashton, an Ashton penalty and a Matt Firth drop-goal. In the second half Cougars, on the back of some intense games, weakened and Eagles grew stronger going on to lead 10-9 before Andy Robinson picked up a pass from James Rushforth to squeeze in at the corner for the crucial try. It was Jason Ramshaw and Mick Durham's last games for the club.
*Team:* 1. Matt Foster, 2. Max Tomlinson, 3. Dave Foster, 4. James Rushforth, 5. Andy Robinson, 6. Paul Ashton, 7. Matt Firth, 8. Phil Stephenson, 9. Simeon Hoyle, 10. Danny Ekis, 11. Oliver Wilkes, 12. Ian Sinfield, 13 Lee Patterson.
Subs: 14. Chris Wainwright, 15.Richard Merville, 16. Mick Durham, 17. Jason Ramshaw.
*Tries:* Matt Foster, Robinson.
*Goals:* Ashton (2), *Drop Goal:* Firth.
*Referee:* Peter Taberner     *Attendance:* 2,500 (est.)

Winger Andy Robinson goes in for the decisive late try in the National League 2 Grand Final at the Halton Stadium against Sheffield Eagles.

# 2. National League Two table and data

## Final Table

| Team | Pl | W | D | L | F | A | Pts |
|---|---|---|---|---|---|---|---|
| Sheffield Eagles | 18 | 13 | 0 | 5 | 644 | 326 | 26 |
| Chorley Lynx | 18 | 13 | 0 | 5 | 584 | 362 | 26 |
| Keighley Cougars | 18 | 13 | 0 | 5 | 488 | 340 | 26 |
| York City Knights | 18 | 11 | 1 | 6 | 576 | 381 | 23 |
| Barrow Raiders | 18 | 11 | 0 | 7 | 546 | 419 | 22 |
| Hunslet Hawks | 18 | 10 | 1 | 7 | 513 | 425 | 21 |
| Swinton Lions | 18 | 8 | 1 | 9 | 445 | 426 | 17 |
| Workington Town | 18 | 4 | 1 | 13 | 393 | 558 | 9 |
| Gateshead Thunder | 18 | 3 | 1 | 14 | 365 | 663 | 7 |
| London Skolars | 18 | 1 | 1 | 16 | 222 | 876 | 3 |

# Arriva Trains Cup
## (Central Group)

| Team | Pl | W | D | L | F | A | Pts |
|---|---|---|---|---|---|---|---|
| Dewsbury Rams | 10 | 7 | 0 | 3 | 232 | 208 | 14 |
| Batley Bulldogs | 10 | 6 | 0 | 4 | 352 | 155 | 12 |
| Keighley Cougars | 10 | 5 | 0 | 5 | 240 | 200 | 10 |
| Hunslet Hawks | 10 | 5 | 0 | 5 | 205 | 237 | 10 |
| London Skolars | 10 | 0 | 0 | 10 | 127 | 503 | 0 |

# 2003 season summary

## All Games

| Played | Won | Drawn | Lost | | For | Against |
|--------|-----|-------|------|---|-----|---------|
| 34 | 24 | 0 | 10 | | 903 | 646 |

*League Only*

| 18 | 14 | 0 | 4 | | 488 | 340 |

*Home*

| 9 | 7 | 0 | 2 | | 288 | 154 |

*Away*

| 9 | 7 | 0 | 2 | | 201 | 186 |

*All Cups and play-off*

| 16 | 10 | 0 | 6 | | 415 | 296 |

## Scoring Statistics in all games

| | |
|---|---|
| Tries | 151 |
| Goals | 143 |
| Drop Goals | 13 |
| Points | 903 |

| | | |
|---|---|---|
| Debutantes | .............................. | 6 |
| Players used | .............................. | 26 |
| Average Home League Attendance | .................... | 961 |
| Gross Home League Attendance | ....................... | 8,651 |
| Most Appearances | Matt Firth ............... | 34 |
| | David Foster .......... | 34 |
| Top Try Scorer | Matt Foster ............. | 18 |
| Top Goal Scorer | Paul Ashton ........... | 75 |
| Top Points Scorer | Paul Ashton ........... | 186 |

# 3. Player statistics

| Player | App | Sub | Try | Goal | DG | Pts |
|---|---|---|---|---|---|---|
| Ashton Paul | 16 | 4 | 7 | 75 | 8 | 186 |
| Durham Michael | 2 | 13 | 1 | 0 | 0 | 4 |
| Ekis Danny | 20 | 11 | 3 | 0 | 0 | 12 |
| Firth Matt | 34 | 0 | 15 | 0 | 5 | 65 |
| Foster David | 34 | 0 | 9 | 0 | 0 | 36 |
| Foster Matt | 23 | 1 | 18 | 0 | 0 | 72 |
| Guck Phil | 2 | 0 | 0 | 0 | 0 | 0 |
| Helliwell Ricky | 11 | 11 | 4 | 0 | 0 | 16 |
| Hannah Chris | 7 | 12 | 0 | 0 | 0 | 0 |
| Hewitt Gareth | 13 | 4 | 6 | 0 | 0 | 24 |
| Hoyle Simeon | 32 | 0 | 9 | 0 | 0 | 36 |
| Kelly Lee | 2 | 2 | 0 | 0 | 0 | 0 |
| Merville Richard | 3 | 20 | 3 | 0 | 0 | 12 |
| Mitchell Adam | 18 | 1 | 5 | 63 | 0 | 146 |
| Parkin Scott | 2 | 1 | 0 | 0 | 0 | 0 |
| Patterson Lee | 18 | 3 | 3 | 0 | 0 | 12 |
| Ramshaw Jason | 28 | 4 | 8 | 0 | 0 | 32 |
| Robinson Andy | 31 | 0 | 15 | 0 | 0 | 60 |
| Rushforth James | 31 | 2 | 11 | 0 | 0 | 44 |
| Sinfield Ian | 27 | 5 | 5 | 0 | 0 | 20 |
| Smith Karl | 20 | 1 | 8 | 0 | 0 | 32 |
| Steel Matt | 1 | 1 | 0 | 0 | 0 | 0 |
| Stephenson Phil | 29 | 0 | 2 | 0 | 0 | 8 |
| Tomlinson Max | 10 | 0 | 3 | 0 | 0 | 12 |
| Wainwright Chris | 7 | 20 | 6 | 0 | 0 | 24 |
| Wilkes Oliver | 31 | 3 | 10 | 5 | 0 | 50 |
| **Totals:** | | | 151 | 143 | 13 | 903 |

*Notes:* Both Matt Firth and Dave Foster were the only ever-present starters with 34 games each. Oliver Wilkes played in every game with 31 starts and three substitute appearances.

One of the Chorley Lynx pack demonstrates on Oliver Wilkes
his part-time occupation of dental technician.

# 4. The under-18 Academy

It was an outstanding season for the newly established Cougars Academy set-up in Division One, the only National League Two side to feature in that division. There were two teams from National League One, Featherstone and Salford, but the rest were from Super League showing the standard of football Cougars had to face not forgetting of course many of these other academies had been long established.

Superbly led by captain Matt Steel Cougars equipped themselves very well in the campaign rarely being outshone by their high-flying opponents in many games the score probably flattering the opposition whose greater experience and size told over the 80 minutes.

In the coming season Cougars are to run two Academy sides to play in the under-21 senior league and in the under-18 junior league. From last year's team Eddie Wilson, Jordan Ross and Colin Pickles have been signed for the under-21s. For the under-18s Tobias Williams, Rob Weir, Michael Hastings, Jason Dubus-Fisher and Shane Walton have been signed.

## 2003 Squad (with appearances)

Jason Battle (10), Alistair Beaumont (3), Scott Bellamy (10), John Carter (11), Jason Dubus-Fisher (14), Andrew Feather (14), Marco Ferrazzano (10), Robert Grey (8), Michael Hastings (14), Peter Hilliam (9), Tom Holland (4), Gareth Holmes (12), Tom Kenna (6), Robert MacDonald (6), Gary McLelland (13), Martin Mower (6), Tom Palmer (6), Chris Parker (4), Colin Pickles (12), Oliver Pursglove (3), James Robinson (10), Jordan Ross (5), Robert Spencer (6), Matthew Steel (14), Adam Webster (14), Robert Weir (14), Tobias Williams (14), Edward Wilson (12).

## Awards

| | |
|---|---|
| Player of the Year | Colin Pickles |
| Man of Steel | Matt Steel |
| Player's Player | Colin Pickles |
| Sponsor's Player | Tobias Williams |
| Clubman of the Year | Gary McLelland |

The 2003 under-18s Junior Academy Squad
Back left to right: Nigel Simpson (Kadtel main sponsor), David Rooke (Ass coach), Ken Feather (Ass Manager), Matthew Steele, Scott Bellamy, Colin Pickles, Michael Hastings, Eddie Wilson, Chris Parker, Jason Dubus-Fisher, Andy Feather, Martin Mower, Tom Kenna, Rob McDonald, Tom Holland, James Robinson, Jason Battle, Marco Ferrazzano, Shane Walton, Rob Grey, Roger Fisher (Ass coach).
Front left to right: Dr David Lawrence (Team Doctor), Alistair Beaumont, Peter Hilliam, Adam Webster, John Carter, Jeremy Crowther (Academy Manager), Rob Weir, Gareth Holmes, Paul Hazelwood (Coach), Tobias Williams.

Academy graduate Matt Steel – now in the first team

# Results

Sat 17 May      Away    Huddersfield Giants     Lost 12-15
*Tries:* McLennan, Williams *Goal:* Hilliam

Sat 24 May      Away    London Broncos Won 25-10
*Tries:* Webster (2), McLennan, Williams *Goals:* Hilliam (2), Holmes
*Drop-Goals:* Feather (3)

Sat 7 June      Home    Salford City Reds       Draw 22-22
*Tries:* Wilson, Feather, Parker *Goals:* Holmes (3)
*Drop-Goals:* Feather (3), Carter

Sun 15 June     Away    Warrington Wolves       Lost 11-40
*Tries:* Hastings, Battle *Goals:* Holmes *Drop-Goal:* Carter

Sun 22 June     Away    Featherstone Rovers     Won 32-18
*Tries:* Feather (2), Webster, Wear, Williams *Goal:* Hilliam (6)

Sat 28 June     Home    Widnes Vikings          Lost 11-40
*Tries:* Ross, Williams *Goal:* Feather *Drop-Goal:* Carter

Sat 5 July      Home    Warrington Wolves       Lost 12-44
*Tries:* Feather, Webster *Goals:* Hilliam (2)

Sat 12 July     Away    Wakefield T Wildcats    Lost 20-28
*(No points scorers information)*

Sat 19 July     Home    Huddersfield Giants     Lost 21-39
*Tries:* Wilson, Webster, Steele *Goals:* Duffy (4) *Drop-Goal:* Duffy

Sun 27 July     Away    Salford City Reds       Lost 22-27
*Tries:* Duffy, McDonald, Feather, Fisher *Goals:* Duffy (4)

Sun 3 Aug       Away    Widnes Vikings          Lost 31-32
*Tries:* Feather (2), McLelland, Pickles, Bellamy, Williams
*Goals:* Weir (3) *Drop-Goal:* Feather

23

Sat 9 Aug        Home    London Broncos        Won 19-16
*Tries:* Steel, Holmes *Goals:* Duffy (4) *Drop-Goals:* Weir (2) Feather

Sat 16 Aug       Home    Wakefield T Wildcats    Lost 25-42
*Tries:* Feather, Weir, Robinson, Steel *Goals:* Duffy (4)
*Drop-Goal:* Weir

Sat 23 Aug       Home    Featherstone Rovers     Lost 20-21
*Tries:* Feather (2), Robinson, Steel *Goals:* Duffy (2)

Sat 6 Sep        Warrington Wolves (P/O)         Lost 16-36
*(No points scorers information)*

# Junior Academy Under-18 – Division One

|                       | Pl | W  | D | L  | F   | A   | Pts |
|-----------------------|----|----|---|----|-----|-----|-----|
| Widnes Vikings        | 14 | 10 | 0 | 4  | 480 | 284 | 20  |
| Huddersfield Giants   | 14 | 10 | 0 | 4  | 540 | 386 | 20  |
| Warrington Wolves     | 14 | 10 | 0 | 4  | 426 | 387 | 20  |
| Salford City Reds     | 14 | 9  | 1 | 4  | 420 | 293 | 19  |
| Wakefield Trinity     | 14 | 9  | 0 | 5  | 432 | 302 | 18  |
| **KEIGHLEY COUGARS**  | **14** | **3** | **1** | **10** | **274** | **396** | **7** |
| Featherstone Rovers   | 14 | 3  | 0 | 11 | 284 | 519 | 6   |
| London Broncos        | 14 | 1  | 0 | 13 | 246 | 535 | 2   |

# 5. Jason Ramshaw

It was particularly fitting and satisfying to see Jason finish his remarkable career at Keighley with a win in the 2003 National League Two Grand Final. No player deserved this more than Jason who has been at Keighley as its talisman of hope in both good times and bad.

Jason had a distinguished rugby league career as a junior with Travellers and Lock Lane amateur clubs which was rewarded by selection for County and International sides. Naturally he came to the attention of professional clubs and it was his dad's old club, Halifax, who won his signature in 1988. Jason went on to feature prominently at Thrum Hall including an appearance in the divisional Grand Final.

A change of coach at Halifax in 1992 saw an end to Jason's career there but his old coach from Thrum Hall, Peter Roe, soon snapped up the young hooker for the team he was building at his new club Keighley Cougars. Jason came initially on trial but such was his impact that his signature was quickly secured in December 1992.

Throughout the next 11 years Jason's name must have frequently been first on the team sheet. He also worked hard in the club's trailblazing community scheme. He appeared in two Grand Finals in the days when the club saw success and then got down and grafted when the club struggled in subsequent seasons.

Jason was elected to Keighley's Hall of Fame, the only player in the then current squad to do so and then in 2002 was awarded a deserved testimonial by the Rugby Football League. Sadly a severe injury to his shoulder meant his appearances that season were limited and so determined to go out on a high he declared the following season to be his last.

And so that led to the almost fairy tale end to Jason's career at Keighley when he came on from the bench and subsequently scored in his last home game then came on to lift the trophy in his last game in that Grand Final at Widnes. Thanks Rammy.

Jason Ramshaw in his first season with the Cougars

# Jason's complete record for Keighley Cougars

## 1992-93

| Date | Pos | Opponents | Ven | Score | Points |
|------|-----|-----------|-----|-------|--------|
| Aug 30 | 9 | Workington Town | H | 18-2 | |
| Sep 6 | 9 | Hunslet | A | 12-28 | |
| Sep 13 | 15 | Nottingham City (Yorks Cup 1) | A | 30-4 | Try |
| Sep 20 | 15 | Barrow | H | 40-10 | |
| Sep 23 | 9 | Wakefield Trinity (Yorks Cup 2) | A | 16-22 | Try |
| Sep 27 | 9 | Dewsbury | A | 13-24 | |
| Dec 13 | 14 | Whitehaven | H | 8-21 | |
| Dec 20 | 9 | Nottingham City | A | 42-2 | 2 Tries |
| Jan 10 | 9 | Workington Town | A | 21-0 | DG |
| Jan 13 | 9 | Doncaster | H | 31-10 | Try |
| Jan 20 | 9 | Blackpool Gladiators | H | 36-4 | |
| Jan 31 | 9 | Highfield (Challenge Cup 1) | H | 86-0 | 2 Tries |
| Feb 7 | 9 | Ryedale York | H | 22-15 | |
| Feb 14 | 9 | Hull KR (Challenge Cup 2) | A | 28-30 | |
| Feb 21 | 9 | Chorley Borough | H | 78-6 | 2 Tries |
| Feb 28 | 9 | Barrow | A | 42-20 | |
| Mar 3 | 9 | Blackpool Gladiators | A | 82-8 | Try |
| Mar 14 | 9 | Dewsbury | H | 33-24 | Try |
| Apr 9 | 9 | Batley | H | 34-10 | |
| Mar 18 | 9 | Hunslet (Premiership) | H | 34-6 | |
| Mar 25 | 9 | Rochdale Hornets (Prem) | A | 18-26 | DG |

*Appearances: 18 plus 3 subs. Scoring: 11 tries, 2 drop-goals = 46 points.*

## 1993-94

| Date | Pos | Opponents | Ven | Score | Points |
|------|-----|-----------|-----|-------|--------|
| Aug 29 | 9 | Barrow | A | 30-22 | Try |
| Sep 5 | 9 | London Crusaders | H | 14-17 | |
| Sep 12 | 9 | Rochdale Hornets | A | 16-14 | |
| Sep 19 | 9 | Dewsbury | H | 30-9 | |
| Oct 31 | 15 | Nottingham City (Regal T 1) | H | 72-12 | |
| Nov 11 | 9 | Carlisle | A | 24-26 | |
| Nov 14 | 9 | Halifax (Regal T 2) | A | 10-19 | Try |
| Nov 21 | 9 | Batley | A | 16-8 | |
| Nov 28 | 9 | Highfield | H | 44-6 | |
| Dec 5 | 9 | Workington Town | H | 4-16 | |
| Jan 2 | 9 | Ryedale York | A | 4-11 | |

27

| Jan 16 | 9 | Oulton (Challenge Cup 1) | H | 68-0 | Try |
| Jan 19 | 9 | Barrow | H | 68-8 | 3 Tries |
| Jan 23 | 9 | Rochdale Hornets | H | 40-12 | |
| Jan 30 | 9 | Batley (Challenge Cup 2) | A | 29-8 | 3 DGs |
| Feb 2 | 9 | Huddersfield | H | 35-10 | Try, DG |
| Feb 6 | 9 | Dewsbury | A | 6-12 | |
| Feb 13 | 9 | Castleford (Challenge Cup 3) | H | 14-52 | |
| Feb 16 | 9 | London Crusaders | A | 10-13 | |
| Feb 20 | 9 | Hunslet | H | 30-10 | |
| Feb 27 | 9 | Doncaster | H | 12-12 | Try |
| Mar 3 | 9 | Whitehaven | A | 10-32 | |
| Mar 9 | 9 | Bramley | A | 48-24 | |
| Mar 13 | 9 | Swinton | A | 20-16 | |
| Mar 20 | 9 | Carlisle | H | 50-12 | |
| Mar 27 | 9 | Batley | H | 6-22 | |
| Mar 31 | 13 | Huddersfield | A | 10-32 | Try |

*Appearances: 26 plus 1 sub. Scoring: 9 tries, 4 drop-goals = 31 points.*

## 1994-95

| Aug 21 | 9 | Whitehaven | H | 38-8 | |
| Aug 28 | 9 | Rochdale Hornets | A | 30-16 | |
| Sep 4 | 9 | Ryedale York | H | 18-18 | |
| Sep 11 | 9 | London Broncos | A | 30-10 | Try |
| Sep 18 | 9 | Dewsbury | H | 46-8 | |
| Sep 25 | 9 | Bramley | A | 18-2 | |
| Oct 2 | 9 | Barrow | A | 24-10 | |
| Oct 9 | 9 | Batley | H | 22-26 | |
| Oct 16 | 9 | Hunslet | H | 66-10 | |
| Oct 30 | 9 | Carlisle | H | 46-14 | |
| Nov 6 | 9 | Whitehaven | A | 38-8 | |
| Nov 13 | 9 | Rochdale Hornets | H | 28-13 | |
| Nov 27 | 9 | Chorley Borough (Regal T 1) | H | 56-0 | Try |
| Dec 4 | 9 | Bramley (Regal T 2) | H | 28-4 | |
| Dec 11 | 9 | Ryedale York | A | 52-12 | 2 Tries |
| Dec 18 | 9 | Sheffield Eagles (Regal T 3) | H | 26-10 | |
| Dec 20 | 9 | Hull KR | H | 24-12 | |
| Dec 31 | 9 | Huddersfield | A | 15-10 | Try, DG |
| Jan 8 | 9 | Warrington (Regal T 4) | H | 18-20 | |

| | | | | | |
|---|---|---|---|---|---|
| Jan 11 | 9 | London Broncos | H | 14-25 | |
| Jan 15 | 9 | Swinton | A | 48-6 | |
| Jan 24 | 9 | Chorley (Challenge Cup 3) | H | 68-0 | Try |
| Feb 1 | 9 | Leigh | H | 38-6 | |
| Feb 6 | 9 | Bramley | H | 24-8 | |
| Feb 12 | 9 | Dewsbury (Challenge Cup 4) | H | 24-12 | |
| Feb 19 | 9 | Barrow | H | 28-6 | |
| Feb 26 | 9 | Huddersfield (Challenge Cup 5) | H | 0-30 | |
| Mar 3 | 9 | Batley | A | 6-8 | |
| Mar 19 | 9 | Hunslet | A | 33-18 | DG |
| Mar 22 | 9 | Dewsbury | A | 2-20 | |
| Mar 26 | 9 | Carlisle | A | 2-12 | |
| Apr 4 | 9 | Leigh | A | 34-13 | Try |
| Apr 9 | 9 | Swinton | H | 42-6 | |
| Apr 14 | 9 | Hull KR | A | 14-6 | Try |
| Apr 17 | 9 | Huddersfield | H | 22-22 | |
| Apr 23 | 9 | Highfield (at Rochdale) | A | 104-4 | 3 Tries |
| May 7 | 9 | Hull KR (Prem 1) | H | 42-16 | |
| May 14 | 9 | London Broncos (Play-off S/F) | H | 38-4 | |
| May 21 | 9 | Huddersfield (Prem Final) | N | 26-6 | 2 DGs |

*Appearances: 39 Scoring: 11 tries, 4 drop-goals = 48 points.*
*\* Only missed one game all season versus Highfield (H) 12 March*

## 1995-96

| | | | | | |
|---|---|---|---|---|---|
| Aug 20 | 9 | Huddersfield | A | 36-26 | Try |
| Aug 27 | 9 | Rochdale Hornets | A | 50-4 | |
| Sep 3 | 9 | Hull | H | 21-12 | |
| Sep 10 | 9 | Dewsbury | H | 44-5 | |
| Sep 20 | 9 | Salford | A | 22-14 | Try |
| Sep 24 | 9 | Whitehaven | H | 58-8 | |
| Oct 1 | 9 | Widnes | A | 16-16 | 2 DGs |
| Nov 1 | 9 | Batley | A | 21-14 | |
| Nov 5 | 9 | Featherstone Rovers | H | 31-0 | |
| Nov 11 | 9 | St Helens (Regal T 2) | H | 14-42 | |
| Nov 19 | 9 | Huddersfield | H | 40-6 | |
| Dec 3 | 9 | Wakefield Trinity | A | 4-16 | |
| Dec 10 | 9 | Salford | H | 6-34 | |

*Appearances: 13 Scoring: 2 tries, 2 drop-goals = 10 points.*

## 1996

| Date | | Opponent | H/A | Score | |
|---|---|---|---|---|---|
| Mar 31 | 9 | Dewsbury | H | 54-2 | 2 Tries |
| Apr 5 | 9 | Rochdale Hornets | H | 14-12 | |
| Apr 8 | 9 | Hull | H | 34-30 | Try |
| Apr 14 | 9 | Huddersfield | A | 12-10 | Try |
| May 26 | 17 | Wakefield Trinity | H | 30-10 | Try |
| Jun 2 | 9 | Salford | H | 8-45 | |
| Jun 9 | 9 | Widnes | A | 12-6 | Try |
| Jun 16 | 8 | Dewsbury | A | 6-14 | |
| Jun 23 | 9 | Rochdale Hornets | H | 42-12 | |
| Jun 30 | 9 | Hull | A | 26-14 | |
| Jul 7 | 9 | Huddersfield | H | 10-37 | |
| Aug 18 | 14 | Widnes | H | 64-12 | Try |
| Aug 25 | 16 | Batley | H | 40-14 | |
| Sep 1 | 16 | Hull | H | 41-28 | DG |
| Sep 8 | 15 | Salford (Div Prem Final) | N | 6-19 | |

*Appearances: 10 plus 5 subs Scoring: 7 tries, 1 drop-goal = 29 points.*

## 1997

| Date | | Opponent | H/A | Score | |
|---|---|---|---|---|---|
| Jan 26 | 9 | Redhill (Challenge Cup 3) | H | 62-4 | Try |
| Feb 9 | 9 | Workington Town (Ch Cup 4) | A | 24-14 | |
| Feb 22 | 9 | Halifax (Challenge Cup 5) | A | 21-8 | |
| Mar 2 | 9 | Workington Town | A | 22-10 | |
| Mar 9 | 9 | St Helens (Challenge Cup 6) | H | 0-24 | |
| Mar 12 | 9 | Hull | H | 8-18 | |
| Mar 16 | 16 | Huddersfield | A | 12-36 | |
| Mar 30 | 9 | Swinton | A | 34-12 | 2 Tries |
| Apr 6 | 9 | Whitehaven | H | 12-21 | |
| Apr 13 | 9 | Hull KR | A | 22-22 | 2 Tries |
| Apr 16 | 15 | Widnes | H | 54-6 | |
| Apr 20 | 9 | Dewsbury | H | 16-26 | |
| Apr 27 | 9 | Wakefield Trinity | A | 42-22 | Try |
| May 11 | 9 | Featherstone Rovers | H | 34-30 | |
| May 18 | 9 | Huddersfield | H | 18-12 | |
| May 23 | 9 | Hull | A | 12-13 | |
| May 26 | 9 | Workington Town | H | 30-10 | Try |
| Jun 1 | 9 | Widnes | A | 12-19 | |
| Jun 15 | 9 | Swinton | H | 26-6 | Try |

| Jun 22 | 9 | Whitehaven | A | 16-12 | |
|---|---|---|---|---|---|
| Jun 29 | 9 | Hull KR | H | 12-4 | Try |
| Jul 4 | 9 | Dewsbury | A | 14-19 | |
| Jul 13 | 9 | Wakefield Trinity | H | 20-18 | Try |
| Jul 20 | 9 | Featherstone Rovers | A | 14-16 | |
| Jul 27 | 9 | Widnes (Prem) | H | 34-16 | |
| Aug 3 | 9 | Rochdale Hornets (Prem) | A | 28-20 | |
| Aug 14 | 9 | Swinton (Prem) | A | 19-15 | |
| Aug 25 | 9 | Rochdale Hornets (Prem) | H | 28-10 | |
| Aug 31 | 9 | Leigh (Prem) | A | 6-20 | |
| Sep 7 | 9 | Swinton (Prem) | H | 36-14 | 2 Tries |
| Sep 14 | 9 | Workington Town (Prem QF) | A | 36-10 | 2 Tries |
| Sep 21 | 9 | Huddersfield (Prem S/F) | H | 8-18 | |

*Appearances: 30 plus 2 subs Scoring: 14 tries= 56 points.*

## 1998

| Feb 1 | 9 | Saddleworth (Challenge Cup 3) | H | 66-16 | 3 Tries |
|---|---|---|---|---|---|
| Feb 8 | 9 | Swinton | A | 16-41 | |
| Feb 15 | 9 | Wigan (Challenge Cup 4) | H | 0-76 | |
| Feb 22 | 9 | Wakefield Trinity | H | 10-14 | |
| Mar 3 | 9 | Rochdale Hornets | A | 16-20 | |
| Mar 8 | 9 | Dewsbury | A | 12-50 | |
| Mar 15 | 9 | Leigh | H | 32-16 | Try |
| Mar 22 | 9 | Whitehaven | A | 12-46 | Try |
| Mar 29 | 9 | Hunslet | H | 22-31 | |
| Apr 10 | 9 | Hull KR | H | 12-20 | |
| Apr 13 | 9 | Featherstone Rovers | A | 2-44 | |
| Apr 19 | 9 | Widnes | H | 25-22 | |
| Apr 26 | 9 | Swinton | H | 20-18 | |
| May 6 | 9 | Wakefield Trinity | A | 0-18 | |
| May 10 | 9 | Rochdale Hornets | H | 50-4 | |
| May 17 | 9 | Dewsbury | H | 22-20 | Try |
| May 24 | 9 | Leigh | A | 30-18 | Try |
| May 31 | 9 | Whitehaven | H | 22-18 | Try |
| Jun 3 | 9 | Hunslet | A | 8-14 | |
| Jul 26 | 16 | Dewsbury | H | 26-10 | |
| Aug 3 | 16 | Wakefield Trinity | A | 16-56 | |
| Aug 7 | 9 | Swinton | H | 18-18 | |
| Aug 16 | 9 | Widnes | A | 30-6 | Try |

| | | | | | |
|---|---|---|---|---|---|
| Aug 21 | 13 | Featherstone Rovers | H | 18-20 | |
| Aug 30 | 13 | Hull KR | A | 17-6 | DG |

*Appearances: 23 plus 2subs Scoring: 9 tries, 1 drop-goal = 37 points.*

## 1999

| | | | | | |
|---|---|---|---|---|---|
| Jan 31 | 9 | Rochdale Mayfield (Ch Cup 3) | H | 48-2 | 3 Tries |
| Feb 7 | 9 | Doncaster | H | 42-16 | |
| Feb 14 | 9 | Widnes (Challenge Cup 4) | A | 20-28 | Try |
| Feb 21 | 9 | Bramley | A | 12-14 | Try |
| Mar 7 | 9 | York | H | 8-10 | |
| Mar 14 | 9 | Dewsbury | A | 8-35 | Try |
| Mar 21 | 9 | Whitehaven | H | 30-16 | Try |
| Apr 2 | 9 | Featherstone Rovers | H | 18-32 | |
| Apr 5 | 9 | Barrow | A | 22-21 | Try |
| Apr 11 | 9 | Widnes | H | 24-22 | |
| Apr 18 | 9 | Leigh | A | 16-28 | Try |
| Apr 25 | 13 | Lancashire Lynx | H | 40-14 | |
| May 9 | 9 | Oldham | H | 32-28 | Try |
| May 16 | 9 | Swinton | A | 15-14 | DG |
| May 23 | 15 | Workington Town | H | 18-22 | |
| Jun 6 | 9 | Hull KR | H | 2-17 | |
| Jun 13 | 9 | Hunslet | A | 8-48 | |
| Jun 20 | 9 | Doncaster | A | 23-18 | DG |
| Jun 23 | 13 | Rochdale Hornets | A | 26-18 | |
| Jun 27 | 9 | Bramley | H | 36-10 | Try |
| Jul 4 | 9 | York | A | 14-24 | |
| Jul 11 | 9 | Dewsbury | H | 24-24 | |
| Jul 18 | 9 | Whitehaven | A | 20-22 | Try |
| Jul 25 | 13 | Rochdale Hornets | H | 30-20 | Try |
| Aug 1 | 13 | Featherstone Rovers | A | 20-40 | |
| Aug 8 | 13 | Barrow | H | 22-20 | Try |
| Aug 15 | 9 | Widnes | A | 16-24 | |

*Appearances: 26 plus 1sub Scoring: 14 tries, 2 drop-goals = 58 points.*

## 2000

| | | | | | |
|---|---|---|---|---|---|
| Jan 16 | 9 | Hull KR | H | 10-24 | |
| Jan 23 | 9 | Featherstone Rovers | A | 20-34 | Try |
| Jan 30 | 9 | Cardiff Cougars (Ch Cup 3) | H | 90-0 | Try |

| | | | | | |
|---|---|---|---|---|---|
| Feb 4 | 9 | Dewsbury | H | 22-6 | |
| Feb 13 | 9 | Villeneuve (Challenge Cup 4) | H | 14-16 | |
| Apr 4 | 9 | York | A | 26-2 | Try |
| May 1 | 9 | Lancashire Lynx | A | 98-4 | 2 Tries |
| May 7 | 9 | Workington Town | H | 54-8 | |
| May 10 | 9 | Oldham | A | 24-14 | Try |
| May 14 | 9 | Batley | H | 40-12 | Try |
| May 21 | 9 | Hull KR | A | 30-8 | |
| May 26 | 9 | Lancashire Lynx | H | 68-0 | Try |
| May 29 | 9 | Leigh | A | 16-26 | Try |
| Jun 4 | 9 | Doncaster Dragons | H | 27-30 | DG |
| Jun 11 | 9 | Rochdale Hornets | A | 30-10 | |
| Jun 18 | 9 | Sheffield Eagles | A | 28-16 | |
| Jun 25 | 9 | Whitehaven | H | 50-12 | 2 Tries |
| Jul 2 | 9 | Swinton | H | 66-12 | 2 Tries |
| Jul 9 | 9 | Doncaster (Prem) | H | 44-22 | Try |
| Jul 23 | 9 | Dewsbury (Prem S/F) | A | 12-38 | |

*Appearances: 19 plus 1sub Scoring: 14 tries, 1 drop-goal = 57 points.*

## 2001

| | | | | | |
|---|---|---|---|---|---|
| Dec 3 | 9 | Hunslet | A | 44-12 | |
| Dec 10 | 9 | Dewsbury | H | 32-6 | |
| Dec 17 | 9 | York | A | 48-14 | |
| Dec 24 | 9 | Gateshead | A | 52-0 | Try |
| Jan 3 | 9 | Hull KR | H | 24-8 | |
| Jan 7 | 9 | Sheffield Eagles | A | 56-16 | |
| Jan 14 | 9 | Featherstone Rovers | H | 22-22 | Try |
| Jan 30 | 9 | Doncaster Dragons | A | 23-17 | DG |
| Feb 25 | 9 | Batley | H | 66-12 | |
| Mar 7 | 9 | Rochdale Hornets | H | 20-23 | |
| Mar 11 | 9 | Workington Town | A | 32-4 | |
| Mar 18 | 9 | Barrow | H | 60-20 | Try |
| Mar 25 | 9 | Widnes | A | 22-19 | Try |
| Apr 1 | 9 | Leigh | H | 6-16 | |
| Apr 8 | 9 | Whitehaven | A | 4-17 | |
| Apr 13 | 9 | Swinton | H | 22-26 | |
| Apr 16 | 9 | Hull KR | A | 10-17 | |
| Apr 22 | 9 | Chorley Lynx | H | 60-12 | |

| Date | | Opponent | | Score | |
|---|---|---|---|---|---|
| Apr 29 | 7 | Oldham | A | 4-38 | |
| May 6 | 9 | Hunslet | H | 26-24 | Try |
| May 9 | 7 | Whitehaven | H | 4-30 | |
| May 13 | 9 | Dewsbury | A | 9-19 | |
| May 27 | 9 | Sheffield Eagles | H | 26-14 | |
| May 30 | 9 | Leigh (Trans-Pen Cup Final) | H | 0-36 | |
| Jun 3 | 9 | Featherstone Rovers | A | 0-42 | |
| Jun 10 | 9 | Doncaster | H | 52-12 | Try |
| Jun 17 | 9 | Batley | A | 14-16 | |
| Jul 1 | 9 | Chorley Lynx | A | 60-10 | 3 Tries |
| Jul 8 | 9 | Featherstone Rovers (P/Off 1) | A | 24-28 | Try |

*Appearances: 29 Scoring: 10 tries, 1 drop-goal = 41 points.*

## 2001-02

| Date | | Opponent | | Score | |
|---|---|---|---|---|---|
| Dec 3 | 9 | Dewsbury | A | 22-25 | |
| Dec 9 | 9 | Chorley | H | 22-16 | |
| Dec 16 | 9 | Workington | A | 18-58 | Try |
| Jan 20 | 9 | Featherstone Rovers | H | 16-36 | |
| Jan 27 | 9 | St Gaudens (Challenge Cup 3) | H | 0-24 | |
| Feb 17 | 9 | Whitehaven | A | 10-24 | |
| Feb 24 | 9 | Gateshead | H | 32-10 | |
| Mar 3 | 9 | Barrow | H | 30-28 | |
| Mar 10 | 9 | Batley | A | 4-56 | |
| Mar 17 | 9 | Hunslet | H | 30-22 | |
| Mar 24 | 9 | Swinton | A | 6-33 | |

*Appearances: 11 Scoring: 1 try = 4 points.*

## 2003

| Date | | Opponent | | Score | |
|---|---|---|---|---|---|
| Jan 19 | 13 | Doncaster (ATC) | H | 21-14 | |
| Jan 26 | 13 | Thornhill Trojans (Ch Cup 3) | H | 33-10 | |
| Feb 3 | 13 | Dewsbury (ATC) | A | 6-12 | |
| Feb 9 | 13 | Sheffield Eagles (Ch Cup 4) | A | 24-25 | |
| Feb 23 | 13 | Hunslet (ATC) | A | 4-16 | |
| Mar 9 | 13 | London Skolars (ATC) | H | 78-18 | 2 Tries |
| Mar 16 | 13 | Dewsbury (ATC) | H | 22-2 | |
| Mar 23 | 13 | Doncaster (ATC) | A | 12-42 | |
| Apr 6 | 13 | Hunslet (ATC) | H | 21-8 | |
| Apr 13 | 13 | Batley (ATC) | A | 16-4 | |
| Apr 18 | 13 | Hunslet | A | 20-12 | |
| Apr 21 | 13 | London Skolars | H | 68-6 | |

| Date | | Opponent | | Score | |
|------|---|----------|---|-------|---|
| May 4 | 13 | Chorley | A | 23-22 | |
| May 11 | 13 | York | H | 38-26 | |
| May 25 | 13 | Workington | A | 44-8 | Try |
| Jun 1 | 13 | Barrow | H | 28-15 | |
| Jun 15 | 13 | Gateshead | H | 52-6 | 2 Tries |
| Jun 22 | 13 | Sheffield Eagles | A | 6-33 | Try |
| Jun 29 | 13 | Swinton | H | 18-15 | |
| Jul 13 | 13 | York | A | 28-48 | |
| Jul 20 | 13 | Chorley | H | 20-23 | |
| Jul 27 | 13 | London Skolars | A | 22-14 | |
| Aug 3 | 13 | Hunslet | H | 18-35 | |
| Aug 10 | 13 | Workington | H | 36-6 | |
| Aug 17 | 13 | Barrow | A | 18-16 | Try |
| Aug 24 | 13 | Sheffield Eagles | H | 10-22 | |
| Aug 31 | 13 | Swinton Lions | A | 19-17 | |
| Sep 7 | 13 | Gateshead | A | 21-16 | |
| Sep 14 | 14 | Hunslet (EPO) | H | 25-12 | |
| Sep 21 | 14 | Barrow (ESF) | H | 35-26 | Try |
| Sep 28 | 17 | Chorley Lynx (FE) | A | 45-12 | |
| Oct 5 | 17 | Sheffield Eagles (Div Final) | N | 13-11 | |

*Appearances: 28 plus 4sub Scoring: 8 tries =32 points.*

Jason in his last game for Cougars in the Divisional Grand Final

# 6. The Keighley Calendar

*A chronological diary of events in the history of the club. Compiled by John Pitchford.*

## January

1st     **1978** Bruce Leek's last game in the 15-15 draw at Batley after 113 games for the club.
**1985** Paul Moses debut in the 18-0 home win over Huddersfield.

2nd     **1954** Derek Hallas's debut in the 21-5 home win over Dewsbury.

3rd     **1942** Mel de Lloyd suspended sine die. Ban lifted in October.
**1953** Terry Hollindrake debut in the 7-11 defeat at Salford.

6th     **1934** The 39-5 victory over Bramley was one of the biggest wins in the clubs history at that time.

7th     **1932** Unchanged team for the 6th consecutive game in loss 8-10 at Castleford.
**1996** New Turner Stand officially opened.

8th     **1995** Best attendance of the season (5,600) as Warrington win Regal Trophy match 20-18. Steve Hall breaks a leg.

9th     **1935** Joe Sherburn played for Yorkshire against Lancashire at Leeds.
**1977** Best attendance of the season (2,646) in the 9-8 victory over Dewsbury.

12th     **1975** Tony Garforth's debut in the 5-13 defeat at home by St Helens.

13th     **1906** Ike Jagger scores record 5 tries in 67-0 home win over Castleford. This record was equalled, but not broken until 18 August 1996.
**1934** Hooker Billy Watson played for England as they beat Australia 19-14 at Gateshead.
**1971** Brian Jefferson kicked six goals for Yorkshire as they beat Lancashire 32-12 at Castleford.

15th     **1995** New record of eight consecutive away wins set in 48-6 win at Swinton.

16th     **1983** David Moll played for GB under-24s v France in Carpentras. Great Britain won 28-23.

17th **1973** Brian Jefferson kicked four goals as Yorkshire beat Cumberland 20-7 at Leeds in the County Championship play-off decider.

19th **1929** Hal Jones played rugby union for Wales versus England at Twickenham.

**2003** Debuts for Ian Sinfield and Ricky Helliwell in the Arriva Trains Cup victory 21-14 over Doncaster.

20th **1934** Rare victory over Warrington 10-3 after delayed start due to late arrival of Warrington due to rail problems at Manchester.

21st **1996** Last game of shortened 1995-96 season due to decision to change to a summer season. Lost away to Featherstone Rovers 30-14.

22nd **1976** Charlie Birdsall signed from Castleford in exchange for Paul Orr.

23rd **1937** First ever radio broadcast from Lawkholme Lane for game versus Swinton. Keighley won 16-3. At half-time, Hal Jones (International) and Joe Sherburn (County) received their caps from chairman Sam Slater.

25th **1934** Club captain Ted Spillane placed on the transfer list at his own request.

26th **1909** Drew 8-8 with the Australian Tourists.

27th **1939** Cyril Halliday sets a record of 156 consecutive appearances.

**1973** Best attendance of the season in Challenge Cup defeat 44-8 against Rochdale Hornets.

**2002** Simeon Hoyle's debut as a substitute in the cup-tie versus St Gaudens. Lost 24-0.

29th **1921** Record away defeat as Hull FC win 80-7. This record stood until 1986.

30th **2000** Record highest score at home in cup tie victory over Cardiff Cougars 90-0.

31st **1993** John Wasyliw kicks his 100th goal of the season in only the 18th game to set a new record for goal-scoring in fewest number of games.

# February

**1st**   **1936** Hal Jones played for Wales against England at Craven Park, Hull. Wales won 17-14.

**2nd**   **1957** Joe Phillips debut in the 4-12 home defeat by Hunslet.

**3rd**   **1968** 7-2 home cup tie victory over Batley ends run of nine consecutive defeats.

**4th**   **1992** Lost to Barrow in cup-tie second replay at Widnes 16-0.

**5th**   **1921** First win for 17 games as 5-0 home victory over Bradford Northern breaks record losing streak. Last win 16 October 1920 over Hunslet.

**7th**   **1948** Beat Risehow & Gillhead, a Cumbrian amateur team in the first round, first leg of the Challenge Cup by 11-0.
**1999** First game of the fourth summer season, a 42-16 victory over Doncaster.

**8th**   **1976** Charlie Birdsall's debut in the 21-10 defeat at Swinton.

**9th**   **1986** Best attendance of the season (1,968) as Leigh win cup-tie 24-2.

**10th**   **1934** Attendance of 14,245 for home cup draw 4-4 with Warrington.
**1985** Ricky Winterbottom's debut. Lost to Runcorn 9-5.

**12th**   **1995** Nick Pinkney breaks his own tries-in-a-season record (31) in the 24-12 home cup victory over Dewsbury. He eventually scored 45 in the season.

**13th**   **1994** Best attendance of the season (5,860) as Castleford win Challenge Cup tie 52-14.

**14th**   **1920** 3-0 win over Bradford was first away win for 34 games since 8-2 victory over Barrow in December 1913. No games were played for most of the First World War.
**1934** Lost replayed first round cup-tie at Warrington 15-9.
**1948** Risehow & Gillhead win second leg of cup-tie 10-2 but Keighley win on aggregate. This was the first game played at Derwent Park by a professional club.
**1988** Best attendance of the season (4,398) as Widnes win cup-tie 16-2.

**15th**   **1996** Nick Pinkney scores a try for England versus France at Gateshead.
**1998** Heaviest ever home defeat as Wigan win cup-tie 76-0. The attendance was the best of the season (4,700).

**16th**   **1975** Stuart Gallacher played for Wales in France.

**1996** Martin Wood and Phil Cantillon play for England in the World Nines in Fiji. Jason Critchley and Gareth Cochrane play for Wales.

17th **1992** Martin Wood's debut in the 18-16 home win over Scarborough Pirates.

21st **1999** Jason Ramshaw sets a new record for tries-in-a-career by a forward of 68. He scored a try in the 14-12 defeat away to Bramley.

22nd **1926** Lost second replay cup-tie against Bradford Northern after drawing 2-2 and 5-5.

23rd **1952** Chris Brereton's last game in the home defeat by Batley 12-10.

**1992** Record score at the time in 70-0 home win over Nottingham City.

24th **1971** Brian Jefferson scored a try and a goal as Yorkshire beat Lancashire 34-8 at Castleford.

**1968** Chairman Norman Mitchell died at game at Widnes.

25th **1975** Stuart Gallacher played for Wales against England at Salford. England won 22-8.

26th **1979** Hull win second round cup-tie 33-12. The attendance of 6,412 was the best of the season.

27th **1991** Jason Lee's debut as a substitute at Halifax. He only played one game for the club but returned in 1998 for a longer spell.

28th **1993** John Wasyliw broke Brian Jefferson's points in a season record of 331 with 2 tries and 7 goals in the 42-20 win at Barrow.

29th **1964** Home victory over Leeds 22-9 ends run of 15 consecutive defeats.

**1984** Jeff Butterfield's debut in the 18-1 home defeat by York.

# March

2nd **1901** First ever game in the cup, a 13-0 home win against Kinsley.

**1935** Record 13th successive home win with 27-7 victory over Dewsbury. Joe Sherburn broke the club points-in-a-season record of 182 scoring two tries and three goals in this game.

3rd **1951** The record attendance of 14,500 set in home cup-tie defeat by Halifax 7-6.

4<sup>th</sup> **1995** Gareth Cochrane played for Great Britain under-21s in France. Great Britain lost 17-16 in Albi.

7<sup>th</sup> **1991** John Wasyliw's debut in the 15-10 home defeat by Workington Town.

8<sup>th</sup> **1992** The best attendance of the season (2,221) saw Huddersfield win 30-16.

9<sup>th</sup> **1907** Sam Stacey equalled the try scoring record with five in the 53-10 home victory over Liverpool.

10<sup>th</sup> **1956** Geoff Crewdson's debut in the home loss against Doncaster 15-14.
**1974** Peter Roe's debut in the 42-2 home victory over Blackpool.

11<sup>th</sup> **1979** Gary Moorby's try scoring debut in the 18-16 win at Batley.
**1990** Record home defeat at the time as York win 70-8.

12<sup>th</sup> **1995** Jeff Butterfield's last game in the 68-0 home victory over Highfield.

14<sup>th</sup> **1976** Keighley beat Leigh 13-7 to reach Challenge Cup semi-final. The attendance of 5,642 was the best of the season.

15<sup>th</sup> **1902** Record crowd of 5,957 saw league champions Broughton Rangers win a first round cup-tie 15-7.

16<sup>th</sup> **1993** John Wasyliw broke Brian Jefferson's goals-in-a-season record (155). His 10 goals in the 80-8 win at Highfield took his tally to 158.

17<sup>th</sup> **1906** Keighley reached the third round of the cup for the first time with a dramatic last minute length of the field try by Ike Jagger in the 5-0 victory at Hull.
**1951** First home defeat for 21 games as Wakefield Trinity won 21-17.
**1985** Ian Bragger's debut in the 25-14 defeat at Carlisle.

18<sup>th</sup> **1967** Brian Jefferson kicked his 100th goal of the season in the 16-12 home loss to Wakefield Trinity.

19<sup>th</sup> **1974** Brian Jefferson broke Joe Phillips' points-in-a-season record (261) with four goals in the 17-4 win at Hunslet. He eventually extended it to 331.

21<sup>st</sup> **1937** Les Mason played for the Dominions XIII against France in Lyons. France won 6-3.
**1951** Sam Stacey died. He is the club's record try-scorer with 155 between 1904 and 1920.

22<sup>nd</sup> **1930** Cliff Burton played for Yorkshire v Lancashire at Rochdale. Lancashire won 18-3.

23<sup>rd</sup> **1951** French referee M. Pascal officiates in home game against Huddersfield. Keighley lost 27-7.
**1966** Geoff Crewdson chosen for Great Britain to tour Australia and New Zealand.

24<sup>th</sup> **1991** Andy Eyres signs for Keighley. Phil and Andy Stephenson's debuts in the 24-21 home victory over Barrow.

25<sup>th</sup> **2001** Martyn Wood's last game for Keighley. His injury in the 22-19 victory at Widnes prevented him playing again that season. He played 213 times for the club plus 4 as a substitute scoring 116 tries, 300 goals and 4 drop goals, totalling 1,068 points.

27<sup>th</sup> **1915** Lost 3-2 to St Helens in extra time in cup-tie. A demonstration against the referee resulted in the ground being suspended for the rest of the season.

28<sup>th</sup> **1935** Norman Foster played for England against France in Paris. The game was drawn 15-15.

29<sup>th</sup> **1902** Harry Myers scores first ever hat-trick of tries for the club in Northern Union (rugby league) in the 26-0 home win over Liversedge.

31<sup>st</sup> **1951** Home loss to Wakefield Trinity 17-12 ends run of 21 consecutive home wins which began with a 7-3 victory over Halifax on 17 December 1949.
**1994** Joe Grima's last game in the 10-32 defeat at Huddersfield. This game, which was played at Leeds Road, was also Peter Roe's last game as coach.
**1996** First league game of first ever summer season. Beat Dewsbury at home 54-2.

# April

1<sup>st</sup> **1988** Ian Fairhurst's last game in the 26-12 home win over Huddersfield after 134 appearances.

2<sup>nd</sup> **1929** Norman Foster's debut in the 14-5 away defeat at Featherstone Rovers.
**1971** Alan Clarkson's debut in a 7-4 defeat at Workington.

3<sup>rd</sup> **1965** Les Thomas played for GB under-24s in Toulouse.

**1976** Lost Challenge Cup semi-final played at Fartown to St Helens 5-4.

4th **1942** Jim Sullivan guested for Keighley in wartime home victory 9-4 over Wakefield Trinity.

**1987** Lowest ever attendance (216) for home win against Fulham 22-9.

**1995** Daryl Powell signs for Keighley.

6th **1980** Mick Hawksworth's debut in 15-3 victory at Huyton 15-3.

7th **1937** Beat Wakefield Trinity 5-3 in the Challenge Cup semi-final replay at Fartown after a 0-0 draw at Headingley in the first game.

8th **1995** Announcement of Super League denies Keighley promotion to top division despite winning the Second Division.

9th **1907** Lost 9-4 to Halifax in Championship semi-final play-off.

**2000** Martin Wood scores his 100th try for the club in the 30-18 win at Widnes.

10th **1935** Len Orchard played for Wales who lost 24-11 to England at Liverpool.

**1943** Beat Leeds in wartime Challenge Cup semi-final first leg 5-3. Lost second leg seven days later 27-0 so Leeds won on aggregate to reach the final.

**1994** Carleton Farrell's last game in the 76-0 home win over Bramley.

12th **1958** Joe Phillips kicked three goals in the 18-9 defeat at Swinton to become the first Keighley player to kick 100 goals-in-a-season.

13th **1954** Terry Hollindrake's first try for the club. He scored two in the 20-10 victory over Wigan. This was Keighley's first ever win against Wigan.

14th **1900** First Northern Union game. Lost at home 5-2 to Manningham.

**1906** Lost in cup semi-final 6-3 to Salford at Warrington.

15th **1902** Harry Myers and Hartley Tempest played for Yorkshire versus Durham & Northumberland.

**1934** Bill Watson played for England versus France.

16th **1965** Geoff Crewdson's 200th game in the 24-0 defeat at Featherstone.

**1972** Dean Raistrick's debut in the 35-12 home defeat by Salford.

17th **1994** John Wasyliw's last game in the 54-2 defeat at Workington. He scored 874 points in only 75 games with 54 tries and 329 goals.

18th **1953** Chris Brereton died.

**1953** Harold Palin sets new goals-in-a-season record of 81.

19th **1991** The *Keighley News* announced a competition to find a new name for the club. Young supporter John-Paul Kelly suggested 'Cougars'.

20th **1974** In the last game of the season Brian Jefferson extends his goals-in-a-season record to 155 during the 31-12 defeat at Leeds.

21st **1956** Terry Hollindrake sets a new points-in-a-season record of 204.

**1976** Joe Bardgett's debut in the 5-3 home defeat by Widnes.

22nd **1972** England under-19s hooker Dean Raistrick signs for Keighley.

23rd **1995** Biggest ever win 104-4 versus Highfield at Rochdale, an all-time record Rugby League away win. Nick Pinkney scored five tries in the game to equal the tries-in-a-game record. Keighley Cougars win Second Division Championship.

25th **1993** John Wasyliw plays and scores in all 31 games of the season setting new records for points-in-a-season (490) and goals-in-a- season (187).

26th **1958** Joe Phillips sets new records for points in a season (261) and goals in a season (111).

27th **1922** Last game in the worst league season in the club's history. The 26-3 defeat at Hull KR is the 31st of the season with four wins and one draw to end in 25th place (out of 26) in the league.

28th **1951** Ken Davies' last game in the 8-8 draw at Batley.

**1985** Jeff Butterfield played in all 32 games of that season.

29th **1984** Kevin Farrell's last game in the 38-14 home defeat by Workington Town after 159 appearances.

30th **1986** Heaviest ever defeat: 92-2 at Leigh.

# May

**1st**   **1979** Alan Dickinson's last game in the 19-11 victory at Whitehaven after 185 games in two spells with the club.

**2000** Martin Wood equals John Wasyliw's goals-in-a-game record of 15 in the 98-4 win at Lancashire Lynx.

**3rd**   **1949** Len Ward played for Yorkshire against Lancashire at Halifax. Yorkshire won 12-3.

**4th**   **1946** Former Keighley player Richard Kendall was a touch judge in the Wembley Challenge Cup final between Wakefield Trinity and Wigan.

**6th**   **1967** Ex-Wakefield Trinity full-back Don Metcalfe was appointed as the new coach.

**2001** Paul Ashton's debut. He scored a try and a goal in the 26-24 home victory over Hunslet.

**8th**   **1937** Lost to Widnes in the Challenge Cup Final at Wembley 18-5.

**1994** Nick Pinkney broke the tries-in-a-season record. His try in the 66-12 defeat in the last game of the season at London was his 31st.

**9th**   **1982** Calvin Wilkes's last game in the 26-2 victory at Doncaster after 149 appearances.

**10th** **1977** Testimonial game for Brian Jefferson's benefit jointly with Bradford's Mick Blacker.

**11th** **1997** Tries-in-a-game record holder Jason Critchley's last game in the 34-30 home win over Featherstone.

**13th** **1993** Nick Pinkney joins Keighley.

**1997** Lee Hanlan played for Ireland versus France in Paris.

**14th** **1995** Beat London Broncos 38-4 at home in the divisional play-off semi-final to qualify for the final at Old Trafford.

**16th** **1969** Former player and Director Joe Phillips died. He joined Keighley in 1957 and scored 516 points in 80 games over three seasons.

**17th** **1953** Lost to Huddersfield in Coronation Cup at Blackpool. This was an out of season competition to help launch a new club in Blackpool.

**18th** **1994** Phil Larder appointed as the new coach.

**19th** **1951** Won a friendly away at Ystradgynlais 24-20.

**1995** Nick Pinkney voted Second Division player of the year at the 'Man of Steel' awards.

21st **1995** Beat Huddersfield 26-6 in the Divisional Premiership Final at Old Trafford to wrap up the most successful season in the club's history.

**1995** New record for most wins in a season (31).

**2000** The 38-8 win at Hull KR sets a new club record of 13 consecutive wins in all games.

25th **1940** First round Yorkshire Cup-Tie at Hull KR cancelled due to at least six Keighley players having to work on war contracts. Tie awarded to Hull KR.

26th **2000** The 68-0 home win over Lancashire Lynx was the 14th consecutive victory and set a new record for wins in all games.

29th **1963** Garfield Owen sets a new goals-in-a-season record (128). Won at Bradford 25-6 in the last game of an extended season due to no games being played in January and February.

# June

2nd **1996** Brendan Hill's last game as Keighley lose at home to Salford 45-8.

7th **1967** Keighley President and former Chairman John Smallwood appointed as Chairman of the Rugby League Council.

**1996** Best attendance of the season (5,427) as Huddersfield win 37-10.

10th **1976** Matt Foster's birthday.

12th **1900** Keighley joined the Northern Union as the Rugby League was then called.

**1906** The Northern Union ruling body voted to reduce the number of players from 15 to 13 at its AGM at the George Hotel in Huddersfield.

13th **1999** Keith Dixon's last game in the 8-48 loss at Hunslet. His try was the 1,063rd point of his Keighley career with 97 tries, 327 goals and one drop goal in 270 appearances including 28 as a substitute.

16th **1989** The signing of Owen Simpson announced.

17th **1972** Phil Stephenson's birthday.

**2001** Oliver Wilkes debut. He scored a try in a 16-14 defeat at Batley.

21st **1959** Albert Eyre signed for Keighley on his 16th birthday.

**1991** Bill Spencer becomes President of the Yorkshire Rugby League.

22<sup>nd</sup> **2003** The 33-6 defeat at Sheffield ended the run of seven successive wins at the start of the league season.

24<sup>th</sup> **1974** James Gillow elected President of the Yorkshire Rugby League.

26<sup>th</sup> **1992** The signing of Joe Grima announced.

**1996** Daryl Powell played for England versus Wales in Cardiff. England won 26-12.

29<sup>th</sup> **1989** Les Coulter takes over as coach and signs Army rugby union winger Owen Simpson. A £2,000 grant received from Bradford Council.

**1997** Daryl Powell's last game in the 12-4 home victory over Hull KR.

30<sup>th</sup> **1996** Nick Pinkney scored his 100th try in only 102 games in the 26-14 home win over Hull. Only the seventh player at the time to score 100 tries for the club.

# July

2<sup>nd</sup> **1990** Tony Fisher and Peter Astbury announced as the new coaching team.

3<sup>rd</sup> **1992** The signing of Ian Gately announced.

4<sup>th</sup> **1986** The *Keighley News* revealed plans to sell the ground and a move to play at Marley.

5<sup>th</sup> **1996** Jason Critchley played for Wales against France in Carcassonne. Wales won 34-14.

13<sup>th</sup> **1991** Steve Hall joins Keighley.

14<sup>th</sup> **1978** Colin Welland become the club President.

15<sup>th</sup> **1986** Colin Dixon and Les Coulter appointed as joint coaches.

18<sup>th</sup> **1974** Rob Valentine and Derek Edwards sign for Keighley.

20<sup>th</sup> **1997** Last league game of the second summer season. Lost away to Featherstone 16-14. A series of eight play-off games followed.

21<sup>st</sup> **1996** André Stoop's last game in the 14-14 draw at Whitehaven.

23<sup>rd</sup> Jason Ramshaw's birthday.

26<sup>th</sup> **1996** Jason Critchley played for Wales against England in Cardiff. England won 26-12.

27<sup>th</sup> **1992** Jason Ramshaw joined Keighley from Halifax.

28<sup>th</sup>  **1995** Keighley take part in the Wigan sevens tournament.
**1996** Keith Dixon scores his 1,000th point for the club with his goal in the 48-26 win at Featherstone.

30<sup>th</sup>  **1976** Terry Morgan, the Great Britain Colts winger joins Keighley.

# August

1<sup>st</sup>  **1971** Beat Hunslet away 17-10 in the Yorkshire Cup first round. The earlier than normal start to the season saw Keighley progress to the semi-finals.

3<sup>rd</sup>  **1980** Beat Doncaster at home 36-22 in a pre-season friendly.

6<sup>th</sup>  **1935** Hooker Cyril Halliday joined Keighley from Huddersfield. He gained one England and seven Yorkshire caps and missed just one club game out of the next 175.
**1976** Beat Wakefield Trinity 24-13 in a pre-season friendly.
**1989** Lost in pre-season friendly 34-10 at Halifax.

7<sup>th</sup>  **1983** Lost at Bradford Northern 19-5 in a pre-season friendly.
**1998** Nathan Antonik's debut and Simon Irving's last game in the 18-18 home draw with Swinton.

9<sup>th</sup>  **1990** Mick Burke joined the club.

10<sup>th</sup>  **1973** John Stephenson signed for Keighley.
**1990** Beat Rochdale Hornets 38-16 in a pre-season friendly at home.

12<sup>th</sup>  **1992** Beat Bradford Northern 26-16 in a pre-season friendly for the Joe Phillips Trophy. New signing Jason Ramshaw played in the game.

13<sup>th</sup>  **1971** Lost Yorkshire Cup semi-final 12-7 at Castleford.
**1989** Lost pre-season friendly 36-22 at home to Bradford Northern.

15<sup>th</sup>  **1936** Dai Davies joined Keighley.
**1993** New signings Nick Pinkney and Greg Austin played in a pre-season 27-21 win over Bradford Northern for the Joe Phillips Trophy.

18<sup>th</sup>  **1959** Record home defeat at the time by Hunslet 36-7.
**1979** Lee Greenwood's debut in a 33-12 defeat at Hunslet.
**1996** Jason Critchley set a new tries-in-a-game record with six in the 64-12 home win over Widnes.

| | |
|---|---|
| 19th | **1961** The first game of the season as Keighley won at Bradford Northern 14-7. |
| 20th | **1978** Kevin Farrell's debut in the 20-5 home win in the Yorkshire Cup over Doncaster. |
| 21st | **1994** Darren Fleary and André Stoop's debuts in the 38-8 home victory over Whitehaven. |
| 22nd | **1999** Best attendance of the season (2,489) saw Keighley beat Leigh 29-14. |
| 23rd | **1934** Beat Bradford Northern at home in the Lazenby Cup friendly 51-0. |
| | **1937** Ted Spillane left Keighley to Join Bramley. |
| 24th | **1963** Terry O'Brien's debut in an 11-5 loss at Warrington. |
| 25th | **1945** First game after the Second World War. Lost at Featherstone 13-10. |
| | **1996** Last game of the first ever summer season. Beat Batley at home 40-14. |
| 26th | **1967** First ever win at Swinton 13-11 after 18 previous visits. |
| 27th | **1973** Best attendance of the season saw 26-4 defeat by Bradford Northern. |
| | **1995** Matt Foster's debut as a substitute in the 50-4 away victory over Rochdale. |
| 28th | **1920** Sam Stacey's last game in the away defeat to Wakefield Trinity 20-10. |
| | **1984** Keith Dixon signs for Keighley. |
| 29th | **1972** John Burke's debut in the home defeat against Bradford 35-13. |
| | **1993** Nick Pinkney's debut in the away win at Barrow 30-22. Also in this game a new record for consecutive league wins was set at 15. |
| 30th | **1992** Debuts for Ian Gately, Joe Grima and Jason Ramshaw in the home victory over Workington Town 18-2. |
| 31st | **1954** New colours of emerald green and scarlet hoops worn for first time in the home game against Huddersfield which was lost 36-26. |

# September

| | |
|---|---|
| 1st | **1906** First game after the number of players was reduced from 15 to 13. |

**1991** Steve Hall and Andy Eyres debuts in the 41-12 home defeat by Bramley.

2nd **1939** Last game before Second World War. Drew at home with Leigh 5-5.

**1950** Lost at home to Castleford in the Yorkshire Cup 14-9 to end run of 13 home wins.

3rd **1978** Graham Beale's debut in the 15-12 defeat at Oldham.

**1989** Best attendance of the season saw Hull KR win 50-16.

4th **1971** Brian Jefferson scored his 2,000th point for the club in the 30-19 defeat at St Helens.

5th **1993** John Wasyliw sets new record of scoring in 46 consecutive games.

6th **1918** First game after First World War lost at Halifax 23-2.

**1952** First television broadcast from Keighley who lost to the Australian Tourists 54-4.

7th **1963** Alan Dickinson's debut in the 9-5 home defeat by Halifax in the Yorkshire Cup.

**1980** Ian Fairhurst's debut in the 45-6 defeat at Rochdale.

**2003** Cougars finish third in the National League Two level on points with leaders Sheffield Eagles.

8th **1996** Lost 19-6 to Salford in the Divisional Premiership Final at Old Trafford.

9th **1933** New grandstand official opening. Lost to Leeds 9-6.

**1984** Dean Raistrick's last and 186th game in the 21-19 home loss to Carlisle.

10th **1974** Brian Jefferson played for Yorkshire versus Cumbria at Workington. He kicked two goals, but Yorkshire lost 10-7.

**1989** Owen Simpson's debut in the 29-6 loss at Dewsbury.

11th **1957** David Smith and Derek Hallas played at Hull for Yorkshire against Cumberland. Yorkshire won 27-18.

**1994** Simon Irving's debut in the 30-10 win at London Broncos.

12th **1925** David McGoun's debut in the 33-3 home win over Bramley. He is the joint record holder for appearances for the club (372) with Hartley Tempest.

**1973** Brian Jefferson (7 goals, 1 try) played for Yorkshire, who beat Cumbria 37-12 at Bramley.

**1993** Brendan Hill's debut at Rochdale.

14th **1932** Joe Sherburn signs for Keighley from Halifax.

50

**1983** Best attendance of the season (2,503) in home Yorkshire Cup 30-8 defeat by Hull.

15th **1934** Yorkshire beat Villeneuve 26-17 at Lawkholme Lane. Joe Sherburn scored a try for Yorkshire.

**1958** Terry Hollindrake and Derek Hallas played for Yorkshire against Cumberland at Whitehaven. Cumberland won 29-7.

**1982** Dave Jickells's 261st and last game.

16th **1974** Peter Roe and Dean Raistrick played at Widnes for Yorkshire against Lancashire, as Lancashire won the County Championship play-off. Lancashire won the match 29-11.

17th **1932** Joe Sherburn's debut in the 9-9 draw at home to York.

**1977** Brian Jefferson's 300th and last game in the 14-4 home Yorkshire Cup loss to Castleford.

18th **1963** Roy Sabine scored a try for Yorkshire in their 11-5 win over Australia.

**1985** Peter Roe takes over as coach from the ailing Geoff Peggs.

19th **1956** Terry Hollindrake played for Yorkshire against Cumberland at Whitehaven. Cumberland won 15-14.

**1973** Brian Jefferson (3 goals), played for Yorkshire versus Lancashire at Widnes. Lancashire won 17-15.

20th **1921** Lost to Australian Tourists 29-0.

**1992** Darren Appleby's debut. He scored two tries in the 40-10 home win over Barrow.

21st **1901** First ever game against Wakefield Trinity. Won 7-6 at home.

**1997** Ian Gateley's last game in an 18-8 home defeat by Huddersfield.

23rd **1957** David Smith played for Yorkshire against Lancashire at Widnes. Yorkshire won 25-11.

**1970** Terry Hollindrake's last game in the 20-8 defeat at Wakefield Trinity after 233 games with 109 tries and 337 goals. A total of 1,001 points.

24th **1972** Bruce Leek's debut in the 21-13 defeat at York in the Players No.6 Competition.

25th **1963** Roy Sabine played against Cumberland for Yorkshire at Wakefield. Cumberland won 15-13.

51

**1974** Peter Roe and Dean Raistrick played for Yorkshire versus Lancashire at Lawkholme Lane. Yorkshire won 20-14.

**1996** Daryl Powell and Jason Critchley played for Great Britain versus Papua New Guinea President's XIII. Great Britain won 34-8.

26th **1955** Terry Hollindrake scored one try for Yorkshire versus Lancashire at Oldham. Lancashire won 26-10.

**1956** David Smith played for Yorkshire against Lancashire at Hull. Lancashire won 35-21.

27th **1950** Pat Callaghan played for Yorkshire versus Cumberland at Whitehaven. Cumberland won 10-5.

**1952** Roy Bleasby's debut at Castleford.

**1958** Roy Sabine's debut at home to Castleford.

28th **1959** Terry Hollindrake played for Yorkshire versus Australia at York.

**1996** Daryl Powell played for Great Britain versus Papua New Guinea. Great Britain won 32-30.

**2003** Cougars win 45-12 at Chorley to qualify to play Sheffield in the National League Two Final at Widnes.

29th **1951** Record away win at the time at Bramley 53-7.

30th **1979** Best attendance of the season. 5,772 saw a 15-9 home defeat by Bradford Northern in the John Player Trophy.

# October

1st **1929** Lost to Australian Tourists 15-9.

**1930** Cliff Burton played for England versus Other Nationalities at St Helens. England won 31-18.

2nd **1996** Jason Critchley played for Great Britain versus Fiji President's XIII. Great Britain won 42-16.

**1983** Lee Greenwood's last and 153rd game. Lost at Dewsbury 28-18.

3rd **1952** Neville Black joins Keighley from Wigan.

**1885** First official game played at Lawkholme Lane (Rugby Union) versus Liversedge.

5th **1949** Len Ward played for Yorkshire versus Lancashire at Warrington. Lancashire won 22-13.

**1957** Joe Phillips set a new points-in-a-game record (24) in the 39-20 win at Halifax.

**1986** Mick Hawksworth set a new tries-in-a-career record for a forward of 67. His try was in his last full game in the 44-12 defeat at Fulham.

**2003** Cougars win 13-11 over Sheffield in the National League Two Final at Widnes. This was Jason Ramshaw's last game for the club.

6th **1996** Daryl Powell scored two tries for the Great Britain Tourists in the test in Fiji. Great Britain won 72-4.

7th **1911** Joe Hey's debut in the 24-8 home victory over Bramley.

**1995** Daryl Powell played for England versus Australia in the World Cup. England won 20-16

8th **1966** Colin Evans debut in the 19-10 defeat at Halifax.

**1995** Fiji beat South Africa 52-6 at Cougar Park in the World Cup.

9th **1994** Grant Doorey's debut in the 26-22 home defeat by Bramley.

10th **1951** Len Ward played for Yorkshire against Lancashire at Leigh. Yorkshire won 15-5.

**1996** Daryl Powell scored a try for Great Britain versus Red Lion Cup XIII in New Zealand. The game was a 22-all draw.

11th **1972** Brian Jefferson kicked seven goals for Yorkshire versus Lancashire at Castleford. Yorkshire won 32-18.

**1995** Nick Pinkney played for England versus Fiji in the World Cup. England won 46-0.

12th **1935** Joe Sherburn scored a try and a goal for Yorkshire versus Lancashire at Widnes. Lancashire won 16-5.

**1960** Lost Yorkshire Cup semi-final 5-4 to Wakefield Trinity at Odsal.

14th **1979** David Moll's debut in the 15-11 home win over Swinton.

**1989** Terry Manning sold to Featherstone.

**1990** New scoreboard and clock used for first time to replace the one first used in 1934.

**1995** Daryl Powell and Nick Pinkney (two tries) played for England versus South Africa in the World Cup. England won 46-0 at Headingley.

15th **1904** Harry Myers benefit game: a 15-2 home win over Bramley.

**1971** Calvin Wilkes scores two tries on his debut in the 16-13 home loss to Leeds.

**1996** Jason Critchley played for Great Britain versus the New Zealand President's XIII. The New Zealand team won 30-22.

**1999** Jason Lee played for Wales versus Ireland. Ireland won 20-17.

16th **1974** Peter Roe (one try) and Dean Raistrick played for Yorkshire versus Lancashire at Widnes in the County Championship play-off. Lancashire won 29-11.

**1994** Nick Pinkney (five tries) in 66-10 win versus Hunslet equals try scoring record.

17th **1876** The original meeting to form the club was held on this day.

**1903** Sam Stacey's debut in the 5-3 home win over Pontefract.

18th **1953** Neville Black played in France for Other Nationalities.

**1987** Mick Hawksworth's last game in the 19-11 home win over Workington after 173 games.

**1996** Daryl Powell played for Great Britain in New Zealand in the first test. New Zealand won 17-12.

20th **1965** Brian Gaines played for the Great Britain under-24s versus France at Oldham. Great Britain won 12-5.

21st **1995** Nick Pinkney played for England versus Wales in the World Cup semi-final at Old Trafford. England won 25-10.

22nd **1999** Jason Lee played for Wales versus Scotland in Glasgow. Scotland won 36-16.

**2003** Six Keighley players, Jason Ramshaw, Matt Foster, David Foster, Ian Sinfield, Matt Firth and Simeon Hoyle all played for the National League Two representative side coached by Peter Roe which beat the touring New Zealand 'A' team 27-8 at Cougar Park.

23rd **1988** Ian Bragger's last game in the 14-43 defeat at Swinton after 101 appearances and 29 tries.

25th **1975** Richard Moncrieff played for Other Nationalities versus Lancashire at St Helens. Lancashire won 36-7.

**1996** Daryl Powell played for Great Britain in New Zealand in the second test. New Zealand won 18-15.

26th **1968** Geoff Crewdson's last game in the 20-11 home win over Blackpool.

**2003** Oliver Wilkes played for Scotland in the 24-22 loss to Ireland in Glasgow.

27<sup>th</sup>  **1951** Lost the Yorkshire Cup final to Wakefield Trinity 17-3.

**1991** Johnny Walker scored a try on his debut in the 42-4 win at Nottingham.

28<sup>th</sup>  **1973** Ken Loxton's debut in the away loss 27-8 to Featherstone in the Captain Morgan Trophy.

**1995** 1,000 children on 'Cougar Convoy' to Wembley for the World Cup Final.

29<sup>th</sup>  **1932** Billy Watson played for Yorkshire versus Lancashire. Yorkshire won 30-3.

31<sup>st</sup>  **1953** Bert Cook equalled the goals-in-a-game record of 11 in the 49-10 home win over Hull Kinston Rovers.

**1993** John Wasyliw set a new points-in-a-game record of 36 with four tries and ten goals in the 72-12 home win over Nottingham in the Regal Trophy.

# November

1<sup>st</sup>  **1977** Barry Seabourne appointed as the new coach.

**1992** A new club record score set in the 86-0 home win over Nottingham. John Wasyliw kicked fifteen goals in the game to set a new goals-in-a-game record.

**1996** Daryl Powell played for Great Britain in the 32-12 third test defeat in New Zealand.

2<sup>nd</sup>  **1907** Sam Stacey (two tries) and Arthur Wilkinson played for Yorkshire versus Lancashire at Halifax. Yorkshire won 15-11.

**1975** Stuart Gallacher played for Wales versus New Zealand.

3<sup>rd</sup>  **1906** Harry Myers fatally injured in the 8-5 victory at Dewsbury.

**1956** Beat Whitehaven 26-23 at home despite being 21-3 down after 20 minutes.

4<sup>th</sup>  **1984** Best attendance of the season (1,570) in the home win over Dudley Hill in the John Player Special Trophy.

**1990** Greg Hiley's debut in the 32-18 home victory over Chorley.

5<sup>th</sup>  **1907** Lost to New Zealand Tourists 9-7.

6<sup>th</sup>  **1975** Stuart Gallacher played for Wales in the 23-2 win over France.

**1977** Best attendance of the season (2,895) saw Leigh win a John Player Trophy game 9-5.

7th   **1910** Sam Stacey played for Yorkshire versus Lancashire at Wigan. Lancashire won 17-3.

**1968** Brian Jefferson played for England versus Wales at Salford. Wales won 24-17.

10th   **1991** John Wasyliw set a new points-in-a-game record of 26 in the 42-14 home win over Highfield.

**2003** Oliver Wilkes played for Scotland kicking two goals in the 8-4 victory over France in Narbonne.

11th   **1922** Richard Kendall's debut in the 14-5 home defeat by Featherstone.

**1959** Fred Ward (one try) played for Yorkshire versus Lancashire at Leigh. Yorkshire won 38-28.

**1974** Terry O'Brien announces his retirement.

**1983** David Moll played for Great Britain under-24s who beat France 28-23 in Villeneuve.

12th   **1989** The 34 points scored in the 34-50 defeat at Oldham is the record number scored in a defeat.

13th   **1965** Brian Jefferson's debut as a trialist in the 21-12 home win over Halifax.

**1966** Billy Aspinall's 100th game in the 22-15 loss to Leeds.

14th   **1933** Lost to the Australian Tourists by 14-7.

15th   **1932** Ted Spillane joins Keighley. He was the first colonial player to join the club.

17th   **1906** Lost in the Yorkshire Cup semi-final 21-0 away to Hull Kingston Rovers.

**1951** Australian Lionel Cooper scores 10 tries against Keighley at Fartown as Huddersfield win 48-3.

18th   **1984** Mal Meninga played for St Helens in their home victory over Keighley by 60-8 in the John Player Trophy.

19th   **1932** Ted Spillane's debut in the 19-0 home victory over Huddersfield.

20th   **1937** Ted Spillane rejoins Keighley.

**1938** Keighley were top of the League after 12 wins out of 14 games.

21st   **1982** Allan Clarkson's last game for Keighley in the 24-12 defeat at Wakefield Trinity.

23rd   **1926** Lost to the New Zealand Tourists 21-3.

**1935** Hal Jones played for Wales versus France at Llanelli. Wales won 41-7.

**1970** Dave Garbett scored three tries in the 24-17 home win over Blackpool. This was the first hat-trick by a forward since 1933.

**1980** Best attendance of the season (3,901) saw Hull Kingston Rovers win the John Player Trophy cup-tie 34-16.

24<sup>th</sup> **1936** Idris Towill joins Keighley from Huddersfield.

**1977** Brian Jefferson announces his retirement.

25<sup>th</sup> **1933** Hal Jones's debut in the 22-2 away defeat at Warrington.

27<sup>th</sup> **1943** Lost 5-2 at Bradford Northern in the first leg of the Yorkshire Cup Final.

**1956** The home defeat 12-0 to Wakefield Trinity was the first time Keighley failed to score since 12 September 1953, a sequence of 138 games.

28<sup>th</sup> **1936** Idris Towill's debut in the 33-5 home win over Featherstone Rovers.

29<sup>th</sup> **1981** Alan Clarkson's 250th game in the 20-8 win at Huyton.

30<sup>th</sup> **1957** Terry Hollindrake scored four tries in the 33-0 victory at Doncaster and is then sent off later in the game!

# December

1<sup>st</sup> **1987** Terry Manning signed from Elland ARL.

2<sup>nd</sup> **1933** Hal Jones's home debut in the loss to Leeds 21-10.

**2001** Debuts for Matt Firth and David Foster in the 25-22 loss at Dewsbury. Matt played in every game in the 2001-2 and 2002-3 seasons.

3<sup>rd</sup> **1995** First league defeat for 18 games as Wakefield Trinity win 16-4 at Belle Vue.

4<sup>th</sup> **1943** Drew 5-5 at home to Bradford Northern in the second leg of the Yorkshire Cup Final. Bradford won the cup 10-7 on aggregate.

5<sup>th</sup> **1903** First ever game against Huddersfield. Lost 3-0 at home.

6<sup>th</sup> **1952** Neville Black's debut in the 28-3 home win over Hull KR.

8<sup>th</sup> **1991** The 11-7 win at Whitehaven was the first win in 11 visits since the 11-6 victory in November 1977.

9<sup>th</sup> **1955** Drew with New Zealand Tourists 11-11.

**1996** Best attendance of the season (4,812) saw Salford win at Cougar Park 34-6.

11th **1994** Nick Pinkney's try in the 52-12 home win over York sets a new record for try scoring in eight consecutive games. He totalled 19 tries in the games.

12th **1925** Tommy Pearson played for Yorkshire versus Lancashire at St Helens. Lancashire won by 26-10.

13th **1987** Gary Rose signs from Leeds amateur club Yew Tree.

15th **1906** The run of 18 successive home wins comes to an end with the defeat 9-8 by Halifax.

16th **1973** First and only win to date at Wigan by 14-10 in the John Player Trophy.

**1979** Tony Garforth's last game in the 18-5 home defeat by Whitehaven after 123 games.

17th **1938** Idris Towill scored four tries in the 20-0 home victory over Rochdale Hornets.

**1954** New dressing rooms opened for the visit of the league leaders Oldham who won 15-11.

**1955** Terry Hollindrake played for Great Britain in the third test 28-13 loss to New Zealand at Headingley.

18th **1908** Hal Jones born in Maesteg.

**1983** Rob Proctor's debut in the 30-12 home victory over Doncaster.

19th **1906** Harry Myers died from injuries received in the match at Dewsbury on 3 November 1906.

22nd **1962** The 20-3 win at Whitehaven was the last game played for two months. No games were played until 10 March the following year with 10 games being postponed due to the severe weather.

25th **1909** Keighley played the Williams Brothers, a team from Wales in a seven-a-side game. Keighley won 48-10.

**1958** Beat York away 7-5 in the last game played by the club on Christmas Day.

26th **1990** Best attendance of the season (2,445) saw Halifax win 12-6.

27th **1958** Derek Hallas' last game in the 13-3 win at Dewsbury after 171 appearances and 68 tries.

**1999** After four seasons of 'summer' rugby a partial reversion to winter saw the new season begin with a win at Hunslet by 21-12.

28th **1934** Ted Spillane left the club to join Bradford Northern.

**1959** Albert Eyres' home debut in the 28-5 home victory over Doncaster.

29<sup>th</sup>   **1975** Dean Raistrick sold to Salford.

**1978** Gary Moorby joined Keighley.

31<sup>st</sup>   **1975** Peter Roe sold to Bradford Northern.

Keighley legend Joe Sherburn, who joined the club in
1932, and played in the 1937 Challenge Cup Final.
(Photo: Courtesy Keighley RL Hall of Fame)

60

# 7. A season to remember: 1900

*The club's first Northern Union season by John Pitchford.*

On 12 April 1900, the members of Keighley Rugby Union Club held a meeting to discuss the lack of interest in rugby union in the district. They decided to apply for membership of the Northern Union, as the Rugby League was called in those days. The original 22 clubs that formed the Northern Union had broken away from the Rugby Football Union in 1895, at the famous meeting at the George Hotel, Huddersfield.

By 1900, there were 30 clubs in the Northern Union, in the Premier Division, which was split into a Lancashire Senior Competition of 14 clubs, and a Yorkshire Senior Competition of 16 clubs. A lower division for junior clubs began in 1898 again split into Lancashire Second, and Yorkshire Second Competitions, and it was into this Yorkshire Second Competition that Keighley were elected, at the AGM, on 14 July 1900. The meeting held at the Little Bull Inn at Wakefield also elected Bingley and Otley into the same competition. The competition was split into two sections, Western and Eastern, but the composition of these sections caused many problems, with some clubs being switched from one section to the other, and further changes continued, even during the season. The geographical splitting by having two sections helped the small clubs with the enormous problem of travelling to away games, and as separate leagues were formed in these sections, clubs only played league games against clubs in their own section.

Two days after deciding to change to rugby league, Keighley played Manningham, a senior Northern Union club, in the first ever game of Rugby League at Lawkholme Lane. Manningham won 5-2. The Keighley team on this historic occasion was F. Kendall; O'Donnell, Cullen, Jennison, Saunders; Myers, Caine; Wigglesworth, Tillotson, Kilby, Jacques, Blades, Ackroyd, Routh, Whittingham.

The new season began on 1 September 1900, and the first competitive game for Keighley was a Yorkshire Second Competition match, at Lawkholme, against Sowerby Bridge, which Keighley won 5-0. Before the season started the Rothwell club disbanded leaving the Eastern section with only 10 clubs and it was decided to refer the matter to the County Committee for a decision. The Northern Union County Committee duly met to consider the unwieldy 15-10 club ratio and was not impressed by it. York Melbourne had also appealed to the County Committee about their exclusion from the Second Competition and with a rare example of common sense; both problems were solved by the County Committee suggesting that York Melbourne be admitted to the competition, and that there be 13 clubs in each section. The composition of the clubs in the two sections was intended to be as follows:

61

*West:* Bingley, Birstall, Elland, Heckmondwike, Hebden Bridge, Idle, Keighley, Luddendenfoot, Otley, Sowerby Bridge, Shipley, Todmorden, Windhill.

*East:* Alverthorpe, Dewsbury, Eastmoor, Featherstone, Goole, Kinsley, Kirkstall, Normanton, Ossett, Outwood Church, Pontefract, York, York Melbourne.

The Elland club, who were due to start in the Western section, as they had done in the previous season, were in a state of bankruptcy. They had tried, unsuccessfully, to merge with other clubs, but on 5 September 1900, their effects were sold by auction. Turnstiles, grandstand, pavilion, goalposts and other appliances realised a total of £25. Rothwell, who had played in the Eastern section in 1899-1900 season, had been disbanded and so Kirkstall who had started in the Western section, were moved into the East, even though they had played, and won, their opening game in the West, away to Windhill. This result was expunged from the record. Other clubs were also struggling, Idle were in debt, and after playing only three games of the new season. Luddendenfoot decided to withdraw from the competition, as they were having difficulty raising a side.

On the playing field Keighley had a very successful start to the season, winning seven of their first eight games in the Western section, with home wins over Sowerby Bridge, Otley, Shipley and Bingley plus away victories at Bingley and Birstall, with the solitary defeat away to Heckmondwike, plus a home victory over Shipley in an 'ordinary' game. This was a friendly match and was not included in the League competition. There were quite a number of these games played by all clubs, as leagues were a relatively new thing.

Following Luddendenfoot's withdrawal, Otley were allowed to return to the Western section. They had been moved to the Eastern section to make the balance between East and West more equal, but were most unhappy with this arrangement, and were pleased to return to the West.

At the end of October, Keighley were in second place in the league table with 12 points. Heckmondwike led the table with 16 points from 9 games. Keighley only played one league game in November, a home victory over Bingley, and played three ordinary games at home, of which two were lost. Bingley were desperately short of funds and when they were due to play Shipley on 8 December, both teams arrived at the Cottingley Bridge ground, to find the goalposts had been taken up by the owner of the field, a Mr John Pickles, because they owed him rent. Perhaps this was when the famous rugby league tradition of moving the goalposts began. In December, for Keighley at home, there were league wins over Dewsbury and Hebden Bridge, plus a draw in the ordinary game against Morecambe. In away matches, there were two defeats at Sowerby Bridge and Shipley, plus a victory at Todmorden. So at the end of the year Keighley were in fourth place in the league table, four points behind leaders Shipley, but with a game in hand.

Early in the New Year, the Western Section decided to expunge the records of Luddendenfoot and Birstall "as both clubs were to all intents and purposes disbanded". All points won or lost against them, would be struck from the league table, so that the new 11-team Western Section then read:

|  | P | W | D | L | Pts |
|---|---|---|---|---|---|
| Shipley | 12 | 10 | 0 | 2 | 20 |
| Sowerby Bridge | 11 | 9 | 0 | 2 | 18 |
| Heckmondwike | 12 | 9 | 0 | 3 | 18 |
| Keighley | 12 | 9 | 0 | 3 | 18 |
| Dewsbury | 14 | 8 | 0 | 6 | 16 |
| Hebden Bridge | 11 | 6 | 0 | 5 | 12 |
| Otley | 14 | 5 | 1 | 8 | 11 |
| Todmorden | 12 | 4 | 0 | 8 | 8 |
| Idle | 11 | 2 | 1 | 8 | 5 |
| Bingley | 11 | 2 | 0 | 9 | 4 |
| Windhill | 14 | 2 | 0 | 12 | 4 |

In January Keighley had mixed fortunes in their games, with home wins over Todmorden and Windhill, plus an away win at Otley, but with defeats at home to Heckmondwike and away to Dewsbury. February provided three victories, all away from home at Idle, Hebden Bridge and Windhill. These games proved to be the final games of the league season, due to the withdrawal of clubs from the league.

Some clubs were unable to fulfil league fixtures, and if these games affected the Championship, the points were awarded to their opponents. In other games, which did not affect the Championship, no points were awarded.

The games, which did affect the Championship, were: -
• Bingley versus Shipley (2 points to Shipley)
• Heckmondwike versus Todmorden (2 points to Heckmondwike)
• Todmorden versus Heckmondwike (2 points to Heckmondwike)
• Todmorden versus Sowerby Bridge (2 points to Sowerby Bridge)

Two more ordinary games were played before the end of the season, both resulted in home victories, over Otley and Morecambe.

In March 1901 Keighley entered the Rugby League Challenge Cup (or Northern Union Cup as it was called in those days) for the first time. In Round one on 2 March, they were drawn at home to Kinsley of the Second Competition East and won 13-0. Round two, on 9 March saw Keighley drawn at home to Second Competition East champions-elect York, who had beaten senior club Halifax in Round one. Keighley refused £120 to transfer the tie, and despite the sending-off of the legendary Harry Myers in the game, earned a 5-5 draw in front of a crowd of 5,293. In the replay York had a player sent off but with half-back Grace in brilliant form won 12-0.

It was a very successful first season in rugby league to finish in second place in their only appearance in the Yorkshire Second Competition, as in the following season they were "promoted" to the Yorkshire Senior Competition. The reason for this was that 14 of the leading clubs broke away from the two County Leagues, to form a new Northern Rugby League. History repeated itself in 1996 of course when Super League was introduced but this time Keighley were not so lucky!

The legendary
Harry Myers
(Photo: Courtesy
Keighley RL Hall
of Fame)

Keighley Northern Union Football Club 1901-02
(Yorkshire Senior Competition)
Back left to right: H. Hoyle (trainer), L. Jackson (groundsman), I. Jagger, E.
Pearson, C. Hardacre, C. F. Saunders, H. Holden, G. B. Whitaker (secretary),
W. R. Elgie (president).
Front left to right: E. Dawson, C. Kilbey, J. W. Fearnley, H. Myers (captain),
A. Slater, T. Holmes, A. Pearson.
Front seated: J. S. Simpson, S. Liddemore.
(Photo: Courtesy Keighley RL Hall of Fame)

65

Keighley Northern Union Football Club 1902-03 Management Committee.
Back left to right: J. W. Booth, G. B. Whitaker, B. W. Main, W. Weatherhead,
G. W. Gibson, W. Shuttleworth.
Middle left to right: F. H. Mitchell, H. F. Robson, W. R. Elgie, Capt. P. Cass
(president), L. Greetham (secretary), W. G. Petty, S. Shackleton.
Front left to right: D. Gaunt, T. Robinson, Northern Rugby League Second
Division trophy. J. Harrison, W. S. Pearson.
(Photo: Courtesy Keighley RL Hall of Fame)

# 8. A Decade in profile: 1900-1910

*The club's first decade by the late Eric Lund, former rugby league correspondent of* The Keighley News, *and David Kirkley.*

The Keighley club was not long in making its name in the Northern Union, and in season 1902-03 they topped the second division with 27 wins out of 34 games.

This was the period when great service was being given by players like Bob Walker, Harry Myers, Arthur Pearson, Charlie Caine, Hartley Tempest and others. And it led up to 1906 - the season that that memorable tragedy overtook the club - the death as a result of an accident on the field of play of Harry Myers.

Myers had moved from Bramley to Keighley around 1895 and stayed with them until his death on 19 December 1906. He played for England in a match against Ireland in 1898, his only international appearance. Altogether with Keighley, Myers scored 90 tries and kicked 178 goals.

In his last full season with the club Keighley had their greatest cup season up to that time. They reached the semi-final of the Northern Union Cup for the first time beating Castleford, Egremont, Hull and Featherstone before falling to Salford in the semi-final game at Warrington.

A newspaper reported that "dissatisfaction among the players with regard to terms of payment was the reason for this defeat, and but for this very discreditable piece of business Keighley would have opposed Bradford in the final". Up to that time Keighley had never had a brighter chance of winning the cup, and it is on record that to Harry Myers the turn of events was a very bitter blow.

The team in that semi-final was: Walker; Stacey, Hardwick, Hardacre, Jagger; Myers, Bateson; Bradley, Fearnley, Bairstow, Tempest, Pickles, McNicholas, Blades and Hopkinson.

Walker was the big kicker of the side. He could find touch half the length of the field and he was a powerful tackler. He could kick goals too - in 1906-07 he landed 80 and scored three tries to set up a club points scoring record which stood for more than 20 years.

About that time Keighley were one of the leading teams in the Northern Union Cup competition, and again in 1907-08 they advanced to the third round by virtue of wins over Brookland Rovers and Whitehaven.

Looking back this was a memorable decade in the club's history when, after the upheaval of changing 'codes,' it was a period of consolidation and not inconsiderable success. Sadly it was to be another quarter of a century before they were to reach such heights again.

*The complete results and tables, compiled by John Pitchford*

**1900-1901: Yorkshire Second Competition West**

| Sat-01-Sep-1900 | Sowerby Bridge | H | Sec | W | 5-0 |
|---|---|---|---|---|---|
| Sat-08-Sep-1900 | Heckmondwike | A | Sec | L | 0-9 |
| Sat-15-Sep-1900 | Idle | A | Sec | W | 38-2 |
| Sat-22-Sep-1900 | Shipley | H | O | W | 7-5 |
| Sat-29-Sep-1900 | Bingley | A | Sec | W | 18-0 |
| Sat-06-Oct-1900 | Otley | H | Sec | W | 18-5 |
| Sat-20-Oct-1900 | Shipley | H | Sec | W | 9-6 |
| Sat-27-Oct-1900 | Birstall | A | Sec | W | 14-3 |
| Sat-03-Nov-1900 | Bingley | H | Sec | W | 17-0 |
| Sat-10-Nov-1900 | Heckmondwike | H | O | L | 0-5 |
| Sat-17-Nov-1900 | Bramley | H | O | L | 2-8 |
| Sat-24-Nov-1900 | Holbeck | H | O | W | 5-3 |
| Sat-01-Dec-1900 | Sowerby Bridge | A | Sec | L | 0-5 |
| Sat-08-Dec-1900 | Todmorden | A | Sec | W | 11-0 |
| Sat-15-Dec-1900 | Dewsbury | H | Sec | W | 5-0 |
| Tue-25-Dec-1900 | Shipley | A | Sec | L | 7-9 |
| Wed-26-Dec-1900 | Morecambe | H | O | D | 0-0 |
| Sat-29-Dec-1900 | Hebden Bridge | H | Sec | W | 13-0 |
| Tue-01-Jan-1901 | Todmorden | H | Sec | W | 2-0 |
| Sat-05-Jan-1901 | Dewsbury | A | Sec | L | 0-3 |
| Sat-12-Jan-1901 | Heckmondwike | H | Sec | L | 0-5 |
| Sat-19-Jan-1901 | Otley | A | Sec | W | 3-0 |
| Sat-26-Jan-1901 | Windhill | H | Sec | W | 6-0 |
| Sat-09-Feb-1901 | Idle | A | Sec | W | 20-0 |
| Sat-16-Feb-1901 | Hebden Bridge | A | Sec | W | 10-5 |
| Tue-19-Feb-1901 | Windhill | A | Sec | W | 13-0 |
| Sat-23-Feb-1901 | Otley | H | O | W | 20-3 |
| Sat-02-Mar-1901 | Kinsley | H | NUC1 | W | 13-0 |
| Sat-09-Mar-1901 | York | H | NUC2 | D | 5-5 |
| Wed-13-Mar-1901 | York | A | NUC2r | L | 0-12 |
| Fri-05-Apr-1901 | Morecambe | A | O | W | 6-3 |

**Final table**

|   | P | W | D | L | F | A | Pts |
|---|---|---|---|---|---|---|-----|
| 1 Heckmondwike | 20 | 17 | 0 | 3 | 263 | 49 | 34 |
| **2 KEIGHLEY** | **20** | **15** | **0** | **5** | **195** | **49** | **30** |
| 3 Shipley | 20 | 15 | 0 | 5 | 144 | 61 | 30 |
| 4 Sowerby Bridge | 20 | 15 | 0 | 5 | 130 | 51 | 30 |
| 5 Dewsbury | 20 | 11 | 1 | 8 | 105 | 95 | 23 |
| 6 Hebden Bridge | 18 | 8 | 0 | 10 | 92 | 119 | 16 |
| 7 Otley | 18 | 7 | 1 | 10 | 97 | 97 | 15 |
| 8 Idle | 17 | 4 | 1 | 13 | 39 | 257 | 9 |
| 9 Todmorden | 18 | 4 | 0 | 13 | 100 | 73 | 8 |
| 10 Bingley | 14 | 2 | 1 | 11 | 24 | 134 | 5 |
| 11 Windhill | 19 | 2 | 0 | 17 | 38 | 243 | 4 |

## 1901-02: Yorkshire Senior Competition

| | | | | | |
|---|---|---|---|---|---|
| Sat-07-Sep-1901 | Bramley | A | YSC | W | 9-2 |
| Sat-14-Sep-1901 | Holbeck | A | YSC | D | 2-2 |
| Sat-21-Sep-1901 | Wakefield Trinity | H | YSC | W | 7-6 |
| Sat-28-Sep-1901 | Leeds | H | YSC | D | 4-4 |
| Sat-05-Oct-1901 | Manningham | A | YSC | L | 6-11 |
| Sat-12-Oct-1901 | Dewsbury | H | YSC | L | 0-5 |
| Sat-19-Oct-1901 | Castleford | A | YSC | D | 3-3 |
| Sat-26-Oct-1901 | Normanton | H | YSC | W | 8-7 |
| Sat-02-Nov-1901 | Heckmondwike | H | YSC | W | 18-5 |
| Sat-09-Nov-1901 | York | A | YSC | D | 8-8 |
| Sat-16-Nov-1901 | Goole | A | YSC | W | 10-5 |
| Sat-23-Nov-1901 | Sowerby Bridge | H | YSC | W | 17-9 |
| Sat-30-Nov-1901 | Liversedge | A | YSC | W | 16-3 |
| Sat-07-Dec-1901 | Bramley | H | YSC | W | 6-0 |
| Sat-14-Dec-1901 | Holbeck | H | YSC | D | 0-0 |
| Wed-25-Dec-1901 | Windhill | H | O | L | 3-5 |
| Thu-26-Dec-1901 | Leeds | A | YSC | L | 0-16 |
| Sat-04-Jan-1902 | Dewsbury | A | YSC | D | 5-5 |
| Sat-11-Jan-1902 | Castleford | H | YSC | W | 18-4 |
| Sat-18-Jan-1902 | Normanton | A | YSC | L | 0-7 |
| Sat-25-Jan-1902 | Heckmondwike | A | YSC | W | 7-0 |
| Sat-01-Feb-1902 | York | H | YSC | W | 7-3 |
| Sat-08-Feb-1902 | Goole | H | YSC | W | 3-2 |
| Sat-22-Feb-1902 | Manningham | H | YSC | W | 10-0 |
| Sat-01-Mar-1902 | Wakefield Trinity | A | YSC | L | 0-10 |
| Sat-08-Mar-1902 | Sowerby Bridge | A | YSC | W | 2-0 |

| Sat-15-Mar-1902 | Broughton Rangers | H | NUC1 | L | 7-15 |
| Sat-29-Mar-1902 | Liversedge | H | YSC | W | 26-0 |
| Fri-11-Apr-1902 | Windhill | A | O | W | 13-7 |

## Final table

| | P | W | D | L | F | A | Pts |
|---|---|---|---|---|---|---|---|
| 1 Leeds | 26 | 22 | 2 | 2 | 317 | 63 | 46 |
| 2 Manningham | 26 | 19 | 1 | 6 | 212 | 85 | 37 |
| **3 KEIGHLEY** | **26** | **15** | **6** | **5** | **192** | **117** | **34** |
| 4 Wakefield Trinity | 26 | 15 | 1 | 10 | 258 | 90 | 31 |
| 5 Holbeck | 26 | 13 | 6 | 7 | 138 | 75 | 30 |
| 6 Dewsbury | 26 | 14 | 1 | 11 | 161 | 94 | 29 |
| 7 York | 26 | 15 | 1 | 10 | 187 | 130 | 29 |
| 8 Normanton | 26 | 13 | 2 | 11 | 148 | 140 | 28 |
| 9 Bramley | 26 | 10 | 1 | 15 | 131 | 162 | 21 |
| 10 Castleford | 26 | 9 | 3 | 14 | 115 | 163 | 21 |
| 11 Heckmondwike | 26 | 7 | 3 | 16 | 83 | 227 | 17 |
| 12 Goole | 26 | 5 | 3 | 18 | 94 | 228 | 13 |
| 13 Sowerby Bridge | 26 | 7 | 0 | 19 | 65 | 179 | 12 |
| 14 Liversedge | 26 | 3 | 0 | 23 | 67 | 415 | 6 |

## 1902-3: Second Division

| Sat-06-Sep-1902 | York | A | D2 | D | 3-3 |
| Sat-13-Sep-1902 | Barrow | H | D2 | W | 12-5 |
| Sat-20-Sep-1902 | Millom | H | D2 | W | 7-0 |
| Sat-27-Sep-1902 | Wakefield Trinity | A | D2 | W | 12-10 |
| Sat-04-Oct-1902 | Morecambe | H | D2 | W | 16-0 |
| Sat-11-Oct-1902 | Dewsbury | A | D2 | W | 6-0 |
| Sat-18-Oct-1902 | Brighouse | H | O | D | 0-0 |
| Sat-25-Oct-1902 | Bramley | A | D2 | L | 3-6 |
| Sat-01-Nov-1902 | Rochdale Hornets | H | D2 | W | 11-8 |
| Sat-08-Nov-1902 | Castleford | H | D2 | W | 10-3 |
| Sat-15-Nov-1902 | Normanton | H | D2 | D | 0-0 |
| Sat-22-Nov-1902 | Manningham | H | D2 | W | 15-0 |
| Sat-29-Nov-1902 | Stockport | H | D2 | W | 19-0 |
| Sat-06-Dec-1902 | Lancaster | A | D2 | W | 10-0 |
| Sat-13-Dec-1902 | Leeds | H | D2 | W | 13-2 |
| Sat-20-Dec-1902 | Holbeck | A | D2 | L | 0-8 |
| Thu-25-Dec-1902 | South Shields | H | D2 | W | 3-0 |
| Fri-26-Dec-1902 | Bramley | H | D2 | W | 9-0 |
| Sat-27-Dec-1902 | Birkenhead | H | D2 | W | 8-0 |

| Date | Opponent | | | | Score |
|---|---|---|---|---|---|
| Sat-03-Jan-1903 | York | H | D2 | W | 7-0 |
| Sat-10-Jan-1903 | Barrow | A | D2 | W | 5-0 |
| Sat-24-Jan-1903 | Wakefield Trinity | H | D2 | W | 16-2 |
| Sat-31-Jan-1903 | Morecambe | A | D2 | W | 8-6 |
| Mon-02-Feb-1903 | Millom | A | D2 | W | 2-0 |
| Sat-07-Feb-1903 | Dewsbury | H | D2 | W | 8-0 |
| Sat-14-Feb-1903 | Heckmondwike | H | NUC1 | W | 37-0 |
| Tue-24-Feb-1903 | Manningham | H | NUC2 | W | 12-0 |
| Sat-28-Feb-1903 | Rochdale Hornets | A | D2 | W | 5-0 |
| Sat-07-Mar-1903 | York | H | NUC3 | D | 2-2 |
| Wed-11-Mar-1903 | York | A | NUC3r | L | 9-12 |
| Sat-14-Mar-1903 | Normanton | A | D2 | L | 11-15 |
| Sat-21-Mar-1903 | Manningham | A | D2 | W | 10-0 |
| Sat-28-Mar-1903 | Stockport | A | D2 | W | 13-0 |
| Sat-04-Apr-1903 | Lancaster | H | D2 | W | 2-0 |
| Mon-06-Apr-1903 | Castleford | A | D2 | W | 7-0 |
| Sat-11-Apr-1903 | Leeds | A | D2 | L | 0-19 |
| Mon-13-Apr-1903 | South Shields | A | D2 | W | 5-2 |
| Sat-18-Apr-1903 | Holbeck | H | D2 | W | 12-0 |
| Sat-25-Apr-1903 | Birkenhead | A | D2 | L | 2-3 |

**Final table:**

| | P | W | D | L | F | A | Pts |
|---|---|---|---|---|---|---|---|
| 1. KEIGHLEY | 34 | 27 | 2 | 5 | 270 | 92 | 56 |
| 2. Leeds | 34 | 26 | 1 | 7 | 334 | 98 | 53 |
| 3. Millom | 34 | 22 | 3 | 9 | 238 | 118 | 47 |
| 4. Rochdale H | 34 | 20 | 6 | 8 | 323 | 88 | 46 |
| 5. Holbeck | 34 | 20 | 5 | 9 | 213 | 83 | 45 |
| 6. Barrow | 34 | 22 | 0 | 12 | 230 | 140 | 44 |
| 7. Wakefield T | 34 | 18 | 2 | 14 | 263 | 196 | 38 |
| 8. Bramley | 34 | 16 | 4 | 14 | 179 | 151 | 36 |
| 9. Birkenhead W | 34 | 14 | 6 | 14 | 125 | 140 | 34 |
| 10 Manningham | 34 | 14 | 5 | 15 | 141 | 170 | 33 |
| 11. Lancaster | 34 | 13 | 4 | 17 | 123 | 214 | 30 |
| 12. Normanton | 34 | 12 | 4 | 18 | 160 | 228 | 28 |
| 13. York | 34 | 11 | 4 | 19 | 111 | 190 | 26 |
| 14. South Shields | 34 | 10 | 2 | 22 | 158 | 264 | 22 |
| 15. Castleford | 34 | 9 | 4 | 21 | 105 | 268 | 22 |
| 16. Dewsbury | 34 | 8 | 5 | 21 | 123 | 245 | 21 |
| 17. Morecambe | 34 | 9 | 2 | 23 | 88 | 220 | 20 |
| 18. Stockport | 34 | 5 | 1 | 28 | 69 | 348 | 11 |

## 1903-04: First Division

| | | | | | |
|---|---|---|---|---|---|
| Sat-05-Sep-1903 | Runcorn | H | D1 | L | 2-10 |
| Sat-12-Sep-1903 | Salford | A | D1 | L | 2-24 |
| Sat-19-Sep-1903 | Leigh | H | D1 | D | 0-0 |
| Sat-26-Sep-1903 | Warrington | A | D1 | L | 7-16 |
| Sat-03-Oct-1903 | Batley | H | D1 | D | 7-7 |
| Sat-10-Oct-1903 | Hull | A | D1 | L | 2-19 |
| Sat-17-Oct-1903 | Pontefract | H | O | W | 5-3 |
| Sat-24-Oct-1903 | Hunslet | H | D1 | W | 7-5 |
| Sat-31-Oct-1903 | Widnes | A | D1 | L | 5-8 |
| Sat-07-Nov-1903 | Swinton | H | D1 | W | 8-3 |
| Sat-14-Nov-1903 | Hull Kingston Rovers | A | D1 | L | 3-13 |
| Sat-21-Nov-1903 | Oldham | H | D1 | L | 2-10 |
| Sat-28-Nov-1903 | Halifax | A | D1 | L | 2-7 |
| Sat-05-Dec-1903 | Huddersfield | H | D1 | L | 0-3 |
| Sat-12-Dec-1903 | Bradford | A | D1 | L | 2-8 |
| Sat-19-Dec-1903 | Wigan | H | D1 | D | 5-5 |
| Sat-26-Dec-1903 | Leeds | A | D1 | L | 0-16 |
| Sat-09-Jan-1904 | Salford | H | D1 | D | 2-2 |
| Sat-16-Jan-1904 | Leigh | A | D1 | L | 3-21 |
| Sat-23-Jan-1904 | Warrington | H | D1 | W | 4-0 |
| Sat-30-Jan-1904 | Batley | A | D1 | W | 9-8 |
| Sat-06-Feb-1904 | Hull | H | D1 | W | 9-0 |
| Sat-13-Feb-1904 | Broughton Rangers | H | D1 | D | 0-0 |
| Tue-16-Feb-1904 | Hull Kingston Rovers | H | D1 | D | 0-0 |
| Sat-20-Feb-1904 | Hunslet | A | D1 | L | 0-20 |
| Tue-23-Feb-1904 | Broughton Rangers | H | D1 | L | 0-7 |
| Sat-27-Feb-1904 | Widnes | H | D1 | L | 0-3 |
| Sat-05-Mar-1904 | Swinton | A | D1 | L | 3-19 |
| Sat-12-Mar-1904 | Lancaster | A | NUC1 | W | 8-0 |
| Sat-19-Mar-1904 | Leeds | A | NUC2 | L | 0-13 |
| Sat-26-Mar-1904 | Halifax | H | D1 | W | 8-5 |
| Wed-30-Mar-1904 | Runcorn | A | D1 | W | 7-0 |
| Sat-02-Apr-1904 | Huddersfield | A | D1 | L | 0-11 |
| Mon-04-Apr-1904 | Broughton Rangers | A | D1 | L | 5-11 |
| Sat-09-Apr-1904 | Bradford | H | D1 | L | 7-10 |
| Tue-12-Apr-1904 | Oldham | A | D1 | L | 3-15 |
| Sat-16-Apr-1904 | Wigan | A | D1 | L | 2-25 |
| Sat-23-Apr-1904 | Leeds | H | D1 | W | 13-8 |

**Final table:**

| | P | W | D | L | F | A | Pts |
|---|---|---|---|---|---|---|---|
| 1. Bradford | 34 | 25 | 2 | 7 | 303 | 96 | 56 |
| 2. Salford | 34 | 25 | 2 | 7 | 366 | 108 | 53 |
| 3. Broughton R | 34 | 21 | 4 | 9 | 306 | 142 | 47 |
| 4. Hunslet | 34 | 22 | 1 | 11 | 250 | 157 | 46 |
| 5. Oldham | 34 | 20 | 3 | 11 | 215 | 110 | 45 |
| 6. Leeds | 34 | 19 | 5 | 10 | 211 | 145 | 44 |
| 7. Warrington | 34 | 17 | 3 | 14 | 214 | 153 | 38 |
| 8. Hull K R | 34 | 17 | 2 | 15 | 191 | 167 | 36 |
| 9. Halifax | 34 | 14 | 3 | 17 | 125 | 148 | 34 |
| 10 Wigan | 34 | 11 | 6 | 17 | 177 | 174 | 33 |
| 11. Swinton | 34 | 12 | 4 | 18 | 139 | 215 | 30 |
| 12. Batley | 34 | 12 | 3 | 19 | 139 | 241 | 28 |
| 13. Hull | 34 | 12 | 3 | 19 | 148 | 258 | 26 |
| 14. Widnes | 34 | 11 | 5 | 18 | 126 | 243 | 22 |
| 15. Leigh | 34 | 10 | 5 | 19 | 174 | 250 | 22 |
| 16. Runcorn | 34 | 11 | 2 | 21 | 151 | 245 | 21 |
| **17. KEIGHLEY** | **34** | **8** | **5** | **21** | **129** | **319** | **20** |
| 18. Huddersfield | 34 | 10 | 0 | 24 | 160 | 353 | 11 |

**Season 1904-05: Second Division**

| Sat-03-Sep-1904 | Dewsbury | A | D2 | L | 2-3 |
|---|---|---|---|---|---|
| Sat-10-Sep-1904 | Barrow | H | D2 | L | 3-5 |
| Sat-17-Sep-1904 | Normanton | A | D2 | W | 2-0 |
| Sat-24-Sep-1904 | Huddersfield | H | D2 | L | 0-3 |
| Sat-01-Oct-1904 | Millom | H | D2 | W | 16-0 |
| Sat-08-Oct-1904 | Morecambe | A | D2 | W | 8-5 |
| Sat-15-Oct-1904 | Bramley | H | D2 | W | 15-2 |
| Sat-22-Oct-1904 | Castleford | A | D2 | L | 5-9 |
| Sat-29-Oct-1904 | Rochdale Hornets | H | D2 | W | 20-0 |
| Sun-06-Nov-1904 | Keighley Olcna | H | O | W | 20-2 |
| Sat-12-Nov-1904 | Brighouse | H | D2 | W | 12-3 |
| Sat-19-Nov-1904 | York | A | D2 | L | 7-10 |
| Sat-26-Nov-1904 | Lancaster | H | D2 | W | 20-0 |
| Sat-10-Dec-1904 | Pontefract | H | D2 | W | 26-5 |
| Sat-17-Dec-1904 | Dewsbury | H | D2 | D | 0-0 |
| Sat-24-Dec-1904 | Barrow | A | D2 | L | 0-11 |
| Sat-31-Dec-1904 | Bradford | A | O | L | 3-19 |
| Sat-07-Jan-1905 | Huddersfield | A | D2 | L | 3-7 |

| Sat-14-Jan-1905 | Millom | A | D2 | L | 3-5 |
| Sat-21-Jan-1905 | Morecambe | H | D2 | W | 16-0 |
| Sat-28-Jan-1905 | Bramley | A | D2 | D | 2-2 |
| Sat-04-Feb-1905 | Castleford | H | D2 | W | 22-0 |
| Sat-11-Feb-1905 | Rochdale Hornets | A | D2 | W | 15-7 |
| Sat-18-Feb-1905 | Bramley | A | NUCIn | W | 3-0 |
| Sat-25-Feb-1905 | Brighouse | A | D2 | W | 8-3 |
| Sat-04-Mar-1905 | Salford | H | NUC1 | W | 8-0 |
| Tue-07-Mar-1905 | Normanton | H | D2 | W | 12-5 |
| Sat-11-Mar-1905 | York | H | D2 | W | 23-2 |
| Sat-18-Mar-1905 | Warrington | A | NUC2 | D | 3-3 |
| Tue-21-Mar-1905 | Warrington | H | NUC2r | L | 0-7 |
| Sat-01-Apr-1905 | Pontefract | A | D2 | L | 6-7 |
| Fri-21-Apr-1905 | Lancaster | A | D2 | W | 13-0 |

**Final table:**

| | P | W | D | L | F | A | Pts |
|---|---|---|---|---|---|---|---|
| 1. Dewsbury | 26 | 22 | 2 | 2 | 247 | 48 | 56 |
| 2. Barrow | 26 | 22 | 0 | 4 | 286 | 68 | 53 |
| 3. York | 26 | 18 | 3 | 5 | 205 | 76 | 47 |
| **4. KEIGHLEY** | **26** | **15** | **2** | **9** | **259** | **94** | **46** |
| 5. Huddersfield | 26 | 14 | 2 | 10 | 231 | 143 | 45 |
| 6. Rochdale H | 26 | 11 | 4 | 11 | 154 | 145 | 44 |
| 7. Millom | 26 | 12 | 0 | 14 | 139 | 173 | 38 |
| 8. Pontefract | 26 | 10 | 1 | 15 | 156 | 175 | 36 |
| 9. Castleford | 26 | 9 | 3 | 14 | 104 | 199 | 34 |
| 10 Normanton | 26 | 9 | 1 | 16 | 105 | 228 | 33 |
| 11. Brighouse R | 26 | 8 | 1 | 17 | 111 | 169 | 30 |
| 12. Lancaster | 26 | 8 | 1 | 17 | 106 | 257 | 28 |
| 13. Morecambe | 26 | 7 | 2 | 17 | 88 | 272 | 26 |
| 14. Bramley | 26 | 5 | 2 | 19 | 95 | 239 | 22 |

**1905-06: Northern Rugby League**

| Sat-02-Sep-1905 | Bradford | H | NRL | L | 5-12 |
| Sat-09-Sep-1905 | Castleford | A | NRL | W | 10-0 |
| Sat-16-Sep-1905 | Normanton | H | NRL | W | 29-0 |
| Sat-23-Sep-1905 | Brighouse | A | NRL | W | 10-5 |
| Sat-30-Sep-1905 | Leeds | H | NRL | W | 2-0 |
| Sat-07-Oct-1905 | Huddersfield | H | NRL | W | 9-3 |
| Sat-14-Oct-1905 | Castleford | H | YC1 | W | 30-8 |
| Sat-21-Oct-1905 | Batley | A | NRL | W | 6-0 |

74

| Sat-28-Oct-1905 | Hunslet | A | YC2 | L | 3-37 |
| Sat-04-Nov-1905 | York | A | NRL | W | 14-0 |
| Sat-11-Nov-1905 | Hunslet | H | NRL | L | 0-17 |
| Sat-18-Nov-1905 | Pontefract | H | NRL | W | 3-0 |
| Sat-25-Nov-1905 | Hunslet | A | NRL | L | 5-6 |
| Sat-02-Dec-1905 | Bramley | H | NRL | L | 0-3 |
| Sat-09-Dec-1905 | Halifax | H | NRL | L | 0-5 |
| Sat-16-Dec-1905 | Barrow | H | NRL | W | 7-3 |
| Sat-23-Dec-1905 | Bradford | A | NRL | L | 0-37 |
| Tue-26-Dec-1905 | Morecambe | H | NRL | W | 18-5 |
| Sat-30-Dec-1905 | Bramley | A | NRL | W | 6-3 |
| Sat-06-Jan-1906 | Normanton | A | NRL | W | 3-2 |
| Sat-13-Jan-1906 | Castleford | H | NRL | W | 67-0 |
| Sat-20-Jan-1906 | Huddersfield | H | NRL | L | 5-8 |
| Sat-27-Jan-1906 | Brighouse | H | NRL | W | 11-3 |
| Sat-03-Feb-1906 | Barrow | A | NRL | W | 8-6 |
| Sat-17-Feb-1906 | Castleford | A | NUCIn | W | 21-6 |
| Tue-27-Feb-1906 | York | H | NRL | W | 12-0 |
| Sat-03-Mar-1906 | Egremont | H | NUC1 | W | 13-0 |
| Sat-17-Mar-1906 | Hull | A | NUC2 | W | 5-0 |
| Sat-24-Mar-1906 | Halifax | A | NRL | D | 5-5 |
| Sat-31-Mar-1906 | Featherstone | H | NUC3 | W | 3-0 |
| Tue-03-Apr-1906 | Batley | H | NRL | W | 10-5 |
| Fri-13-Apr-1906 | Leeds | A | NRL | L | 0-32 |
| Sat-14-Apr-1906 | Salford | N | NUCSF | L | 3-6* |
| Mon-16-Apr-1906 | Morecambe | A | NRL | W | 7-0 |
| Sat-21-Apr-1906 | Pontefract | A | NRL | W | 3-0 |

* At Wilderspool Stadium, Warrington.

## Final Table:

| | P | W | D | L | F | A | % |
|---|---|---|---|---|---|---|---|
| 1. Leigh | 30 | 23 | 2 | 5 | 245 | 130 | 80.00 |
| 2. Hunslet | 32 | 25 | 0 | 7 | 370 | 148 | 78.12 |
| 3. Leeds | 34 | 25 | 2 | 7 | 377 | 123 | 76.47 |
| 4. Oldham | 40 | 28 | 2 | 10 | 446 | 125 | 72.50 |
| **5. KEIGHLEY** | **28** | **19** | **1** | **8** | **255** | **160** | **69.64** |
| 6. Wigan | 34 | 22 | 1 | 11 | 441 | 167 | 66.17 |
| 7. Hull K R | 36 | 22 | 3 | 11 | 246 | 218 | 65.27 |
| 8. Broughton R | 34 | 21 | 1 | 12 | 400 | 222 | 63.23 |
| 9. Halifax | 38 | 20 | 8 | 10 | 261 | 232 | 63.15 |

| 10. Runcorn | 30 | 17 | 3 | 10 | 264 | 136 | 61.66 |
|---|---|---|---|---|---|---|---|
| 11. Huddersfield | 30 | 17 | 2 | 11 | 224 | 174 | 60.00 |
| 12. Bradford | 34 | 19 | 2 | 13 | 371 | 199 | 58.82 |
| 13. Swinton | 32 | 17 | 3 | 12 | 203 | 168 | 57.81 |
| 14. St Helens | 30 | 16 | 1 | 13 | 244 | 212 | 55.00 |
| 15. Warrington | 38 | 19 | 3 | 16 | 270 | 184 | 53.94 |
| 16. Wakefield T | 32 | 13 | 4 | 15 | 188 | 262 | 46.87 |
| 17. Hull | 36 | 16 | 1 | 19 | 304 | 220 | 45.83 |
| 18. Salford | 34 | 14 | 3 | 17 | 272 | 270 | 45.58 |
| 19. Pontefract | 28 | 11 | 1 | 16 | 211 | 196 | 41.07 |
| 20. Batley | 34 | 11 | 5 | 18 | 173 | 215 | 39.70 |
| 21. Widnes | 28 | 10 | 2 | 16 | 129 | 242 | 39.28 |
| 22. Dewsbury | 36 | 13 | 2 | 21 | 162 | 252 | 38.88 |
| 23. Bramley | 26 | 9 | 2 | 15 | 126 | 246 | 38.46 |
| 24. York | 34 | 11 | 2 | 21 | 170 | 249 | 35.29 |
| 25. Barrow | 32 | 9 | 4 | 19 | 138 | 324 | 34.37 |
| 26. Normanton | 24 | 4 | 2 | 18 | 50 | 280 | 20.83 |
| 27. Millom | 20 | 3 | 2 | 15 | 77 | 328 | 20.00 |
| 28. Castleford | 20 | 3 | 2 | 15 | 45 | 325 | 20.00 |
| 29. Rochdale H | 32 | 3 | 6 | 23 | 105 | 327 | 18.75 |
| 30. Morecambe | 26 | 2 | 4 | 20 | 99 | 282 | 15.38 |
| 31. Brighouse R | 26 | 3 | 2 | 21 | 87 | 333 | 15.38 |

## 1906-07: Northern Rugby League

| Sat-01-Sep-1906 | Bradford | A | NRL | L | 0-23 |
|---|---|---|---|---|---|
| Sat-08-Sep-1906 | York | H | NRL | W | 21-5 |
| Sat-15-Sep-1906 | Batley | H | NRL | W | 20-10 |
| Sat-22-Sep-1906 | Bramley | H | NRL | W | 32-3 |
| Sat-29-Sep-1906 | Victoria R | H | F | W | 18-5 |
| Sat-06-Oct-1906 | Liverpool City | A | NRL | W | 32-2 |
| Sat-13-Oct-1906 | New Blackpool | H | YC1 | W | 34-2 |
| Sat-20-Oct-1906 | Barrow | A | NRL | D | 10-10 |
| Sat-27-Oct-1906 | York | H | YC2 | W | 34-2 |
| Sat-03-Nov-1906 | Dewsbury | A | NRL | W | 8-5 |
| Sat-10-Nov-1906 | Bradford | H | NRL | W | 12-10 |
| Sat-17-Nov-1906 | Hull Kingston Rovers | A | YCSF | L | 0-21 |
| Tue-20-Nov-1906 | St Helens | H | NRL | W | 15-5 |
| Sat-24-Nov-1906 | St Helens | A | NRL | L | 9-18 |
| Sat-01-Dec-1906 | Barrow | H | NRL | W | 25-8 |
| Sat-08-Dec-1906 | Huddersfield | H | NRL | W | 28-10 |
| Sat-15-Dec-1906 | Halifax | H | NRL | L | 8-9 |

| Tue-25-Dec-1906 | Batley | A | NRL | L | 10-14 |
| Sat-29-Dec-1906 | Dewsbury | H | NRL | W | 19-8 |
| Tue-01-Jan-1907 | Halifax | A | NRL | L | 0-17 |
| Sat-05-Jan-1907 | York | A | NRL | W | 19-8 |
| Sat-12-Jan-1907 | Hull Kingston Rovers | A | NRL | L | 5-17 |
| Sat-09-Feb-1907 | Bramley | H | NRL | W | 37-7 |
| Sat-16-Feb-1907 | Rochdale Hornets | H | NRL | W | 12-8 |
| Sat-23-Feb-1907 | Batley | H | F | W | 7-5 |
| Sat-02-Mar-1907 | Huddersfield | A | NRL | W | 12-8 |
| Sat-09-Mar-1907 | Liverpool City | H | NRL | W | 53-10 |
| Sat-16-Mar-1907 | Brooklands R | H | NUC1 | W | 18-0 |
| Sat-23-Mar-1907 | Whitehaven Rec | A | NUC2 | W | 14-0 |
| Fri-29-Mar-1907 | Rochdale Hornets | A | NRL | W | 16-6 |
| Sat-30-Mar-1907 | Swinton | A | NUC3 | L | 8-22 |
| Tue-02-Apr-1907 | Hull Kingston Rovers | H | NRL | W | 28-10 |
| Sat-06-Apr-1907 | Halifax | A | ChSF | L | 4-9 |

## Final table:

| | Pl | W | D | L | F | A | % |
|---|---|---|---|---|---|---|---|
| 1. Halifax | 34 | 27 | 2 | 5 | 649 | 229 | 82.33 |
| 2. Oldham | 34 | 26 | 1 | 7 | 457 | 227 | 77.94 |
| 3. Runcorn | 30 | 23 | 0 | 7 | 546 | 216 | 76.66 |
| **4. KEIGHLEY** | **24** | **17** | **1** | **6** | **431** | **231** | **72.91** |
| 5. Wigan | 34 | 23 | 1 | 10 | 656 | 278 | 69.11 |
| 6. Leeds | 30 | 19 | 2 | 9 | 424 | 301 | 66.66 |
| 7. Hunslet | 32 | 21 | 0 | 11 | 520 | 354 | 65.62 |
| 8. Warrington | 34 | 21 | 1 | 12 | 554 | 304 | 63.23 |
| 9. Broughton Rangers | 30 | 17 | 1 | 12 | 496 | 235 | 58.33 |
| 10. Salford | 32 | 18 | 0 | 14 | 462 | 349 | 56.25 |
| 11. Barrow | 26 | 13 | 1 | 12 | 333 | 356 | 51.92 |
| 12. Widnes | 20 | 9 | 1 | 10 | 221 | 320 | 47.50 |
| 13. Hull K R | 32 | 15 | 0 | 17 | 390 | 366 | 46.87 |
| 14. Dewsbury | 28 | 12 | 1 | 15 | 393 | 377 | 44.64 |
| 15. Leigh | 28 | 12 | 1 | 15 | 318 | 311 | 44.64 |
| 16. Wakefield Trinity | 28 | 12 | 1 | 15 | 348 | 409 | 44.64 |
| 17. Swinton | 32 | 14 | 0 | 18 | 308 | 380 | 43.75 |
| 18. Bradford | 30 | 12 | 2 | 16 | 387 | 367 | 43.33 |
| 19. Huddersfield | 32 | 13 | 0 | 19 | 469 | 477 | 40.62 |
| 20. Rochdale Hornets | 26 | 9 | 1 | 16 | 292 | 312 | 36.53 |
| 21. Batley | 24 | 8 | 1 | 15 | 228 | 326 | 35.41 |
| 22. St Helens | 26 | 9 | 0 | 17 | 374 | 353 | 34.61 |

| | | | | | | | |
|---|---|---|---|---|---|---|---|
| 23. Hull | 32 | 11 | 0 | 21 | 337 | 515 | 34.37 |
| 24. York | 24 | 5 | 0 | 19 | 217 | 514 | 20.83 |
| 25. Bramley | 20 | 1 | 0 | 19 | 85 | 466 | 5.00 |
| 26. Liverpool City | 30 | 0 | 0 | 30 | 76 | 1398 | 0.00 |

Pontefract resigned from the league after 8 matches and their record was expunged from the table. Their record was as follows: -

| P | W | D | L | F | A | % |
|---|---|---|---|---|---|---|
| 8 | 3 | 0 | 5 | 63 | 154 | 37.5 |

A top four play-off was introduced for the first time to decide the championship. The top club played the fourth, and the second met the third with the higher placed club having ground advantage. The final was played at a neutral venue.

## Season 1907-08: Northern Rugby League

| | | | | | |
|---|---|---|---|---|---|
| Tue-03-Sep-1907 | St Helens | H | NRL | W | 12-3 |
| Sat-07-Sep-1907 | Ebbw Vale | H | NRL | W | 26-3 |
| Sat-14-Sep-1907 | Halifax | A | NRL | L | 0-7 |
| Sat-21-Sep-1907 | Hunslet | A | NRL | L | 5-15 |
| Sat-28-Sep-1907 | Hull Kingston Rovers | H | NRL | W | 5-2 |
| Sat-12-Oct-1907 | Wakefield Trinity | A | NRL | W | 7-3 |
| Sat-19-Oct-1907 | Huddersfield | H | NRL | W | 14-8 |
| Sat-26-Oct-1907 | Bramley | H | NRL | W | 22-3 |
| Sat-02-Nov-1907 | Bradford | A | NRL | L | 6-14 |
| Tue-05-Nov-1907 | New Zealand | H | Tour | L | 7-9 |
| Sat-09-Nov-1907 | Hull | A | YC1 | L | 10-21 |
| Sat-16-Nov-1907 | Dewsbury | H | NRL | W | 12-8 |
| Sat-23-Nov-1907 | Victoria R | H | F | W | 19-2 |
| Sat-30-Nov-1907 | Bramley | A | NRL | W | 9-5 |
| Tue-03-Dec-1907 | Leeds | H | NRL | W | 12-7 |
| Sat-07-Dec-1907 | York | H | NRL | W | 21-7 |
| Sat-14-Dec-1907 | Batley | H | NRL | W | 9-0 |
| Sat-21-Dec-1907 | Hull | A | NRL | L | 3-24 |
| Wed-25-Dec-1907 | Hull Kingston Rovers | A | NRL | L | 4-10 |
| Thu-26-Dec-1907 | Leigh | H | NRL | W | 8-5 |
| Sat-28-Dec-1907 | Barrow | H | NRL | W | 9-8 |
| Sat-11-Jan-1908 | Wakefield Trinity | H | NRL | W | 33-10 |
| Sat-18-Jan-1908 | York | A | NRL | L | 9-12 |
| Sat-25-Jan-1908 | St Helens | A | NRL | L | 3-11 |

| Sat-01-Feb-1908 | Halifax | H | NRL | L | 12-15 |
|---|---|---|---|---|---|
| Sat-08-Feb-1908 | Hunslet | H | NRL | W | 7-2 |
| Sat-15-Feb-1908 | Batley | A | NRL | L | 5-28 |
| Sat-22-Feb-1908 | Dewsbury | A | NRL | L | 10-16 |
| Sat-29-Feb-1908 | Runcorn | A | NUC1 | L | 5-12 |
| Sat-07-Mar-1908 | Huddersfield | A | NRL | L | 10-40 |
| Sat-21-Mar-1908 | Barrow | A | NRL | L | 3-8 |
| Sat-28-Mar-1908 | Leeds | A | NRL | D | 5-5 |
| Sat-04-Apr-1908 | Bradford | H | NRL | W | 10-5 |
| Tue-14-Apr-1908 | Hull | H | NRL | W | 14-6 |
| Sat-18-Apr-1908 | Ebbw Vale | A | NRL | L | 10-13 |
| Sat-25-Apr-1908 | Leigh | A | NRL | L | 5-53 |

**Final table:**

| | P | W | D | L | F | A | % |
|---|---|---|---|---|---|---|---|
| 1. Oldham | 32 | 28 | 2 | 2 | 396 | 121 | 90.62 |
| 2. Hunslet | 32 | 25 | 1 | 6 | 389 | 248 | 79.68 |
| 3. Broughton R | 30 | 23 | 1 | 6 | 421 | 191 | 78.33 |
| 4. Wigan | 32 | 23 | 1 | 8 | 501 | 181 | 73.43 |
| 5. Halifax | 34 | 22 | 1 | 11 | 483 | 275 | 66.17 |
| 6. Hull K R | 32 | 21 | 0 | 11 | 460 | 307 | 65.62 |
| 7. Warrington | 30 | 18 | 3 | 9 | 431 | 156 | 65.00 |
| 8. Wakefield Trinity | 32 | 20 | 1 | 11 | 422 | 322 | 64.06 |
| 9. Salford | 32 | 19 | 3 | 10 | 344 | 187 | 64.06 |
| 10. Batley | 32 | 20 | 0 | 12 | 360 | 306 | 62.05 |
| **11. KEIGHLEY** | **32** | **17** | **1** | **14** | **320** | **356** | **54.68** |
| 12. Bradford N | 32 | 17 | 0 | 15 | 313 | 350 | 53.12 |
| 13. Runcorn | 30 | 15 | 0 | 15 | 255 | 219 | 50.00 |
| 14. Barrow | 32 | 15 | 0 | 17 | 244 | 272 | 46.87 |
| 15. Huddersfield | 32 | 14 | 1 | 17 | 439 | 330 | 45.31 |
| 16. Hull | 34 | 15 | 0 | 19 | 349 | 323 | 44.11 |
| 17. Rochdale H | 30 | 13 | 0 | 17 | 232 | 290 | 43.33 |
| 18. Dewsbury | 32 | 13 | 1 | 18 | 290 | 358 | 42.18 |
| 19. Leigh | 30 | 11 | 1 | 18 | 279 | 362 | 38.33 |
| 20. Leeds | 32 | 10 | 1 | 21 | 270 | 397 | 32.81 |
| 21. Swinton | 30 | 9 | 1 | 20 | 180 | 316 | 31.66 |
| 22. York | 30 | 9 | 0 | 21 | 284 | 437 | 30.00 |
| 23. Merthyr Tydfil | 30 | 8 | 1 | 21 | 229 | 400 | 28.33 |
| 24. Widnes | 30 | 6 | 4 | 20 | 179 | 335 | 26.66 |

| | | | | | | | |
|---|---|---|---|---|---|---|---|
| 25. St Helens | 32 | 7 | 3 | 22 | 228 | 500 | 26.56 |
| 26. Ebbw Vale | 30 | 6 | 2 | 22 | 153 | 426 | 23.33 |
| 27. Bramley | 32 | 5 | 1 | 26 | 188 | 674 | 17.18 |

## 1908-09: Northern Rugby League

| | | | | | |
|---|---|---|---|---|---|
| Sat-05-Sep-1908 | Dewsbury | A | NRL | W | 5-3 |
| Sat-12-Sep-1908 | Barry | H | NRL | W | 31-0 |
| Sat-19-Sep-1908 | Bramley | H | NRL | W | 49-0 |
| Sat-26-Sep-1908 | Hull Kingston Rovers | A | NRL | D | 10-10 |
| Sat-03-Oct-1908 | York | H | NRL | W | 15-5 |
| Sat-10-Oct-1908 | Hunslet | H | YC | L | 6-14 |
| Sat-17-Oct-1908 | Hull | H | NRL | W | 14-13 |
| Sat-24-Oct-1908 | Wakefield Trinity | A | NRL | L | 3-35 |
| Sat-31-Oct-1908 | Runcorn | H | NRL | L | 5-6 |
| Sat-07-Nov-1908 | Barrow | H | NRL | W | 23-14 |
| Sat-14-Nov-1908 | Huddersfield | A | NRL | L | 8-9 |
| Sat-21-Nov-1908 | Batley | H | NRL | L | 7-8 |
| Sat-28-Nov-1908 | Barry | A | NRL | W | 23-3 |
| Sat-05-Dec-1908 | Wakefield Trinity | H | NRL | W | 21-6 |
| Sat-12-Dec-1908 | Halifax | H | NRL | L | 3-8 |
| Sat-19-Dec-1908 | Huddersfield | H | NRL | L | 0-11 |
| Sat-26-Dec-1908 | Runcorn | A | NRL | L | 5-22 |
| Fri-01-Jan-1909 | Halifax | A | NRL | L | 7-41 |
| Sat-02-Jan-1909 | Bradford | A | NRL | W | 8-2 |
| Sat-09-Jan-1909 | Leeds | A | NRL | L | 5-30 |
| Sat-16-Jan-1909 | Barrow | A | NRL | L | 0-10 |
| Sat-23-Jan-1909 | Leeds | H | NRL | W | 15-0 |
| Tue-26-Jan-1909 | Australia | H | Tour | D | 8-8 |
| Sat-30-Jan-1909 | Hunslet | H | NRL | L | 3-12 |
| Sat-06-Feb-1909 | Hull Kingston Rovers | H | NRL | L | 4-5 |
| Sat-20-Feb-1909 | Bramley | A | NRL | L | 9-10 |
| Sat-27-Feb-1909 | Pemberton | A | NUC | W | 41-6 |
| Sat-13-Mar-1909 | Wigan | A | NUC | L | 0-47 |
| Sat-20-Mar-1909 | Hull | A | NRL | L | 12-16 |
| Wed-24-Mar-1909 | York | A | NRL | L | 0-3 |
| Sat-27-Mar-1909 | Dewsbury | H | NRL | W | 17-7 |
| Sat-03-Apr-1909 | Bradford | H | NRL | W | 27-8 |
| Fri-09-Apr-1909 | Hunslet | A | NRL | L | 7-34 |
| Sat-10-Apr-1909 | Batley | A | NRL | L | 2-24 |

**Final table:**

| | P | W | D | L | F | A | % |
|---|---|---|---|---|---|---|---|
| 1. Wigan | 32 | 28 | 0 | 4 | 706 | 207 | 87.50 |
| 2. Halifax | 34 | 28 | 1 | 5 | 526 | 174 | 83.82 |
| 3. Oldham | 32 | 26 | 0 | 6 | 488 | 176 | 81.25 |
| 4. Batley | 32 | 23 | 3 | 6 | 412 | 176 | 76.56 |
| 5. Huddersfield | 34 | 21 | 3 | 10 | 504 | 292 | 66.17 |
| 6. Wakefield T | 31 | 20 | 1 | 10 | 471 | 318 | 66.12 |
| 7. Salford | 32 | 20 | 1 | 11 | 455 | 309 | 64.06 |
| 8. Merthyr Tydfil | 18 | 11 | 1 | 6 | 184 | 156 | 63.88 |
| 9. Broughton R | 32 | 19 | 1 | 12 | 420 | 330 | 60.93 |
| 10. Warrington | 32 | 18 | 2 | 12 | 473 | 266 | 59.37 |
| 11. Runcorn | 28 | 16 | 1 | 11 | 271 | 191 | 58.92 |
| 12. Hunslet | 32 | 18 | 1 | 13 | 361 | 299 | 57.81 |
| 13. Hull | 34 | 19 | 1 | 14 | 487 | 366 | 57.35 |
| 14. Ebbw Vale | 24 | 12 | 1 | 11 | 249 | 269 | 52.08 |
| 15. Leeds | 32 | 15 | 1 | 16 | 398 | 355 | 48.43 |
| 16. Hull K R | 32 | 14 | 1 | 17 | 429 | 423 | 45.31 |
| 17. St Helens | 28 | 11 | 3 | 14 | 312 | 421 | 44.64 |
| 18. York | 32 | 13 | 1 | 18 | 394 | 510 | 42.18 |
| 19. Dewsbury | 30 | 12 | 1 | 17 | 350 | 324 | 41.66 |
| **20. KEIGHLEY** | **30** | **12** | **1** | **17** | **338** | **355** | **41.66** |
| 21. Leigh | 28 | 11 | 0 | 17 | 214 | 308 | 39.28 |
| 22. Swinton | 32 | 11 | 1 | 20 | 258 | 440 | 35.93 |
| 23. Bradford N | 32 | 11 | 0 | 21 | 324 | 451 | 34.37 |
| 24. Mid-Rhondda | 18 | 5 | 1 | 12 | 111 | 214 | 30.55 |
| 25. Rochdale H | 30 | 8 | 2 | 20 | 195 | 384 | 30.00 |
| 26. Barrow | 32 | 9 | 1 | 22 | 245 | 507 | 29.69 |
| 27. Widnes | 28 | 6 | 3 | 19 | 197 | 359 | 26.78 |
| 28. Treherbert | 18 | 4 | 1 | 13 | 81 | 212 | 25.00 |
| 29. Barry | 18 | 3 | 0 | 15 | 76 | 445 | 16.66 |
| 30. Bramley | 26 | 3 | 0 | 23 | 162 | 582 | 11.53 |
| 31. Aberdare | 17 | 1 | 0 | 16 | 134 | 406 | 5.88 |

## 1909-10: Northern Rugby League

| | | | | | |
|---|---|---|---|---|---|
| Sat-04-Sep-1909 | Wakefield Trinity | H | NRL | W | 5-2 |
| Sat-11-Sep-1909 | Hunslet | A | NRL | L | 2-14 |
| Sat-18-Sep-1909 | Bramley | A | NRL | W | 10-0 |
| Sat-25-Sep-1909 | Leeds | H | NRL | L | 8-12 |

| | | | | | |
|---|---|---|---|---|---|
| Sat-02-Oct-1909 | Hull | A | NRL | L | 10-20 |
| Sat-09-Oct-1909 | Barrow | H | NRL | W | 39-9 |
| Sat-16-Oct-1909 | Dewsbury | A | NRL | W | 14-5 |
| Sat-23-Oct-1909 | Treherbert | H | NRL | W | 20-3 |
| Sat-30-Oct-1909 | Wakefield Trinity | H | YC2 | D | 8-8 |
| Wed-03-Nov-1909 | Wakefield Trinity | A | YC2r | L | 3-7 |
| Sat-06-Nov-1909 | Halifax | A | NRL | W | 18-9 |
| Sat-20-Nov-1909 | Bramley | H | NRL | W | 18-6 |
| Sat-27-Nov-1909 | Treherbert | A | NRL | W | 6-3 |
| Sat-04-Dec-1909 | Halifax | H | NRL | W | 5-0 |
| Sat-11-Dec-1909 | Hull | H | NRL | L | 3-7 |
| Sat-18-Dec-1909 | Wakefield Trinity | A | NRL | L | 6-37 |
| Tue-28-Dec-1909 | Batley | A | NRL | L | 0-10 |
| Sat-01-Jan-1910 | Hull Kingston Rovers | A | NRL | W | 6-0 |
| Sat-08-Jan-1910 | Leeds | A | NRL | L | 10-19 |
| Sat-15-Jan-1910 | Huddersfield | H | NRL | L | 0-6 |
| Sat-05-Feb-1910 | York | A | NRL | W | 17-10 |
| Sat-12-Feb-1910 | Bradford Northern | H | NRL | W | 25-11 |
| Sat-19-Feb-1910 | Hull Kingston Rovers | A | NRL | W | 9-4 |
| Sat-26-Feb-1910 | Broughton Rangers | H | NUC1 | W | 5-0 |
| Sat-12-Mar-1910 | Runcorn | A | NUC2 | W | 5-3 |
| Sat-19-Mar-1910 | Leeds | H | NUC3 | L | 4-7 |
| Sat-26-Mar-1910 | Dewsbury | H | NRL | W | 34-13 |
| Mon-28-Mar-1910 | Barrow | A | NRL | W | 6-3 |
| Tue-29-Mar-1910 | Bradford Northern | A | NRL | W | 14-0 |
| Sat-02-Apr-1910 | Hunslet | H | NRL | W | 30-0 |
| Sat-09-Apr-1910 | Huddersfield | A | NRL | L | 10-11 |
| Sat-16-Apr-1910 | York | H | NRL | W | 47-19 |
| Sat-23-Apr-1910 | Batley | H | NRL | W | 10-9 |

**Final table:**

| | P | W | D | L | F | A | % |
|---|---|---|---|---|---|---|---|
| 1. Oldham | 34 | 29 | 2 | 3 | 604 | 184 | 88.23 |
| 2. Salford | 31 | 24 | 1 | 6 | 387 | 210 | 79.03 |
| 3. Wigan | 30 | 23 | 1 | 6 | 545 | 169 | 78.33 |
| 4. Wakefield T | 32 | 24 | 0 | 8 | 435 | 242 | 75.00 |
| **5. KEIGHLEY** | **28** | **19** | **0** | **9** | **382** | **242** | **67.85** |
| 6. Leeds | 34 | 21 | 1 | 12 | 451 | 317 | 63.26 |
| 7. Warrington | 34 | 20 | 2 | 12 | 408 | 252 | 61.76 |

| | | | | | | | |
|---|---|---|---|---|---|---|---|
| 8. Huddersfield | 34 | 21 | 0 | 13 | 477 | 301 | 61.76 |
| 9. Halifax | 34 | 21 | 0 | 13 | 395 | 269 | 61.76 |
| 10. St Helens | 31 | 18 | 2 | 11 | 468 | 367 | 61.29 |
| 11. Hull K R | 35 | 19 | 1 | 15 | 410 | 376 | 55.71 |
| 12. Leigh | 32 | 15 | 5 | 12 | 218 | 206 | 54.68 |
| 13. Hull | 36 | 19 | 0 | 17 | 456 | 373 | 52.77 |
| 14. Batley | 33 | 16 | 2 | 15 | 313 | 201 | 51.51 |
| 15. Hunslet | 32 | 16 | 0 | 16 | 321 | 347 | 50.00 |
| 16. Runcorn | 30 | 14 | 1 | 15 | 232 | 317 | 48.33 |
| 17. Ebbw Vale | 24 | 9 | 2 | 13 | 156 | 211 | 41.66 |
| 18. Widnes | 28 | 10 | 3 | 15 | 152 | 244 | 41.07 |
| 19. Rochdale H | 32 | 13 | 0 | 19 | 272 | 371 | 40.62 |
| 20. Dewsbury | 30 | 11 | 1 | 18 | 253 | 338 | 38.33 |
| 21. Swinton | 30 | 10 | 2 | 18 | 203 | 306 | 36.66 |
| 22. Broughton R | 34 | 10 | 2 | 22 | 295 | 498 | 32.35 |
| 23. Bradford N | 34 | 9 | 1 | 24 | 176 | 388 | 27.94 |
| 24. York | 30 | 6 | 1 | 23 | 269 | 473 | 21.66 |
| 25. Bramley | 29 | 6 | 0 | 23 | 181 | 532 | 20.68 |
| 26. Barrow | 28 | 5 | 1 | 22 | 146 | 377 | 19.64 |
| 27. Merthyr Tydfil | 21 | 2 | 1 | 18 | 94 | 354 | 11.90 |
| 28. Treherbert | 12 | 0 | 0 | 12 | 55 | 289 | 0.00 |

During a game in around 1909 between Keighley and Huddersfield at
Lawkholme Lane, the scrum collapses and a Huddersfield player looks to
be taking drastic action to stop Sam Stacey getting away with the ball.
(Photo: Courtesy Keighley RL Hall of Fame)

# 9. Game of the decade

*A contemporary report from* The Keighley News.

## Saturday 18 April 1903:

### *KEIGHLEY WIN THE CHAMPIONSHIP*

#### KEIGHLEY 12 - HOLBECK 0

#### A SPLENDID VICTORY OVER HOLBECK

#### REMARKABLE DAY OF ENTHUSIASM

Five thousand people last Saturday saw Keighley discharge their last home league game of the season; saw the "ALL WHITES" exact full compensation for that eight points victory which Holbeck gained at their expense last December saw the Keighley men preserve their unbeaten record for the Lawkholme ground this season and what was of far more importance, saw the Keighley men secure that distinction they had fought so valiantly and so brilliantly for since last September – the Championship of the Second Division of the Northern League, with its consequent promotion to the senior league.

Keighley entered the fray on Saturday with three points lead in the statistical table, and though their supporters had little doubt of their ability to pull off the remaining home game and thus make their position as leaders absolutely secure, there was the possibility, in the event of their failing on Saturday and in the final game of the programme at Birkenhead, and Leeds succeeding in their last two games of the season, Keighley being deprived of the Championship.

The confidence of the Lawkholme teams supporters in the ability of their team was, fortunately, not misplaced, for while Keighley were trouncing Holbeck, Millom were very kindly putting Leeds "through the mill" and the two results in combination had the effect of increasing Keighley's lead in the competition to five points, and thereby settling in decided fashion the destiny of the Championship honours for the season 1902-03.

85

Saturday was a proud day for the Keighley team and their large and loyal following, and it was peculiarly appropriate that the Championship should have been gained on the birthday of the clubs popular president (Mr C.P Cass). It was a brilliant day for so important a meeting and the ground was in capital condition. Mariner's Band played selections prior to the match. About the ground were ranged sheets for contributions on behalf of Chris Hardacre, the popular Keighley centre who is hospital with a broken leg, sustained in the Lancaster match.

Holbeck turned out as selected for the match, but on the Keighley side, Lord came into the three-quarter line in the absence of Holmes, who had not received his permit, and Slater and Liddemore were in the forwards in place of Fearnley and Dawson. The full teams were as below: -

*Keighley:* A. Pearson, Lord, Sharpe, Jagger, Myers, Caine, Holden, Hall, F. Pearson, Kilby, Tempest, Royston, Liddemore, Slater.

*Holbeck:* Snowden, Leonard, Duxbury, Bowen, Steele, Kelly, Wilkinson, Sanders, Blades, Dawson, Hupton, Hainstock, Sutcliffe, Thorpe, Taylor.

Myers started for Keighley against the slope and wind, and from the first it was palpably apparent that the "All Whites" meant business. Myers was particularly in evidence, and immediately after the start his judicious use of touch took play to the Holbeck line, where the defenders had a warm time of it for the first 15 minutes. They, however, met the Keighley attacks with great resoluteness, stopping Myers, Caine and Jagger a few yards from the line in rapid succession. At length Keighley's persistency was rewarded, for Caine, getting hold from a scrummage in the Holbeck goalmouth, dropped a pretty goal. On the re-start mis-fielding gave Holbeck a footing near the Keighley line and Kelly tried to equalise by dropping at goal, but without success. The home backs, again using the touchline with certainty and regularity brought the game back into the Holbeck quarter, but could not manage to cross. Then the visitors were penalised, and Myers placed the ball for a shot at goal and his attempt was successful. There was no further incident of note up to half time, with the exception of a fine burst by Kelly. The teams crossed over with Keighley leading by two goals to nothing. In the second half the Keighley men again took up the running, but their chances at first went all wrong and nothing resulted, the defence of

86

the visitors again being effective. At length Caine tried and failed with another drop at goal and Leonard ran the ball out in preference to saving. Walker replied to this effort with a well judged kick and from the ensuing scrummage Caine passed out to Myers and he to Sharpe and the latter cleverly engineered an opening for his wing man, Arthur Pearson, to run over, Myers, took the kick at goal and made no mistake about it. After the restart the Holbeck forwards replied with a rattling dribble half the length of the field, and Duxbury still further improved matters with a good run, but the effort was not sustained, and the home players were almost immediately back into the Holbeck quarters. Here Snowden, the visiting full back, sprained his right ankle in kicking dead, and had to be taken off the field. Afterwards Keighley scored again, Myers starting the movement with a strong burst from the scrummage, his pass went to Sharpe, and the latter again judged the situation to a nicety, and when he did pass on to Pearson the wing man had practically a clear course. Myers missed the shot at goal. There was no further scoring and the game ended with the score

**Keighley:** Three goals, two tries – 12 Points
**Holbeck:** Nil

### *"See the conquering heroes Comes"*

After the match, Marriners Band escorted the Keighley team from the field to the headquarters (The Wellington Hotel) by way of Lawkholme Lane, North Street and Low Street, playing "see the conquering heroes comes" en route. The utmost enthusiasm was displayed, cheering being indulged in again and again by the crowd. The demonstration almost equalled in vigour that which marked the return of the Keighley team from Mytholmroyd in season 1896-97 after winning the Championship of the second competition.

# Appendix : Representative honours

**Great Britain:** T. Hollindrake, D. Powell.
**Great Britain Tourists:** H. Jones, G. Crewdson, D. Powell, J. Critchley
**England:** C. Burton, W. Watson, N. Foster, B. Jefferson, N. Pinkney, D. Powell.
**Wales:** W. Jones, H. Jones, L. Orchard, C. Evans, S. Gallacher, J. Critchley, J. Lee
**Scotland:** O. Wilkes
**Ireland:** L. Hanlan
**France:** R. Pastre-Courtine
**Other Nationalities:** N. Black, R. Valentine, R. Moncreiff
**Great Britain under-24:** B. Gaines, D. Moll, L. Thomas
**Great Britain under-21:** G. Cochrane
**England under-24:** L. Thomas

**Yorkshire:** I. Jagger, A. Pickering, H. Myers, H. Tempest, S. Stacey, A. Wilkinson, J. Winterburn, B. Holmes, T. Pearson, C. Burton, W. Watson, J. Sherburn, N. Foster, A. Burnell, L. Ward, P. Callaghan, T. Hollindrake, D. Hallas, D. Smith, F. Ward, R. Sabine, B. Jefferson, P. Roe, D. Raistrick.

**Cumberland:** C Taylor

*Miscellaneous*
**Rugby League XIII:** W. Watson, N. Foster
**Dominions XIII:** L. Mason
**Army XIII:** K. Davies
**British Services:** R. Bleasby, M. Bell.
**England Services:** D. Hallas.
**Yorkshire League:** W. Watson.
**Great Britain Academy Presidents XIII:** D. Larder.
**Northern Rugby League XIII:** R. Lloyd.
**Tourists Rugby League XIII:** G. Crewdson.
**Northern Ford Premiership under-21:** D. Ekis.
**National League Two Representative:** J. Ramshaw, M. Foster, I. Sinfield, M. Firth, D. Foster, S. Hoyle.

For details of all our Rugby League
books and publications, to order the
latest edition of **Our Game** (£2.50 post
free), and a free catalogue, write to:

## London League Publications Ltd
## PO Box 10441
## London E14 0SB


**Or**


## Visit our website:


# www.llpshop.co.uk

# *A Dream Come True*
## *A Rugby League Life*
## By Doug Laughton
## with Andrew Quirke

Doug Laughton is one of the key figures in British Rugby League in the last 40 years.

His playing career started at St Helens in 1962. He then moved to Wigan and captained them in the 1970 Challenge Cup Final.

A further move followed to Widnes, with more success, including four Wembley finals.

He also captained Great Britain and was a member of the last British Lions team to beat the Australians.

As a coach, he won every trophy in the game with Widnes, including a memorable World Club Challenge victory over Canberra in 1989. He signed Jonathan Davies and Martin Offiah for Widnes. He managed Leeds from 1991 to 1995, which included two more Wembley finals.

This hard hitting book covers his full career and will be of interest to all Rugby League fans.

Published in October 2003 in hardback at £14.95.
Available from all good bookshops, (ISBN: 1903659124)
or post free from London League Publications Ltd, PO Box 10441, London E14 0SB.
Cheques to London League Publications Ltd.
Credit card orders via our website: www.llpshop.co.uk